Perspective

Learning to See the Business World Through the Eyes of a Cultural Anthropologist

John Mirocha, Ph.D.

Copyright 2011 John Mirocha, Ph.D.
All Rights Reserved
Printed in the United States of America

ISBN-13:978-1466323391
ISBN-10:1466323396

This book has been developed by Dr. John Mirocha, a cultural anthropologist who has worked in the business management, academic and consulting communities for more than thirty years. This book is about who we are and how we perceive, think and interact with the business world around us. Because it has been developed from the experience of a cultural anthropologist, it might be a bit unusual in its format and content. Our hope is that it will be refreshing. This guide provides you with new ideas, insights and skills to manage in today's fast paced, complex, global, business world.

This book is copyrighted material. All rights reserved. It is unlawful to copy this material in any way (beyond the copying permitted by Section 107 and 108 of the U.S. Copyright Law and except by reviews for the public press), without written permission in advance from John Mirocha & Associates, Inc. No part of this publication can be reproduced, stored in a retrieval system, or transmitted in any form or by any means, electronic, mechanical, photocopying, recording or otherwise, without prior written permission of the author.

© Copyright 2011 John Mirocha & Associates, Inc.
www.johnmirocha.com

What are readers saying about <u>Perspective</u>?

The book is much more than a Personal Working Guide. *Perspective* is a critical read for all who are interested in leadership development, increasing self-understanding and improving business performance. The five insights drawn from anthropology are essential for all leaders and consultants. "Remember, a map is not just a map; it is a view of the world," and *Perspective* is not just book, it is the way by which you read the map.

The stories, vignettes, and examples poignantly shape *Perspective*. Significantly, the conclusions include not only the author's perspective, but the readers' as well – this is what perspective is about.

–Richard Bents, Ph.D. President, Future Systems Consulting, Inc. and Partner with ShareOn Corporate Leader Resources

As an HR Business Partner for a Fortune 500 health care company, Dr. Mirocha's book is an invaluable resource. Through my work supporting senior leadership in the organization with their divisional operations initiatives, the anthropologist perspective framework that is provided is not only critical in application to how I can more effectively support and develop the leadership teams I work with, but it is also an implementation tool for HR professionals to use in guiding teams through leadership development, change management, and organization cultural awareness. The vignettes Dr. Mirocha uses to exemplify and highlight the conceptual themes in each chapter are not only effective as a metaphor to the learning objectives, but they also serve as a first-hand account of his experiences as seen through the lens of a cultural anthropologist, each complete with lessons learned as a capstone.

—Jinah Chernivec, HR Business Partner, Davita

Perspective provides a valuable, often overlooked view of approaching the business world. Dr. Mirocha masterfully weaves concepts, stories that bring those concepts to life, and reflection questions to enable leaders to move into a new, very useful way of approaching their challenges.

—Amy Cullen Rivera, Manager, Organization and Professional Development, Noblis

As John Mirocha so brilliantly points out, it is **perspective** that we all crave. The degree and intensity of change today can be numbing and disorienting. This book serves as a guide to help you sort the significant from the trivia and the truth from whim. It offers skill building exercises to increase your ability to adapt, thrive and lead in new ways that will bring more energy, clarity and confidence to your work. Through entertaining and enlightening stories, John reveals the methods of a cultural anthropologist – observe with an open heart, keep lists of lessons learned and trust that inspiration, discipline and focus will produce needed insights. As John so wisely states "Perspective is not about keeping up. It is about finding and staying on the forefront, even daring to create it." You have taken the complex and made it simple, relevant and timeless.

—Brenda Hanson Dickinson, Dean of Continuing Education and Customized Training, Normandale Community College

Among the many business books written each year this book stands out for taking the perspective of a cultural anthropologist and applying it to everyday leadership and management challenges. The many stories such as those which illustrated "the center of the universe is not in your backyard" and "you are part of the system" make the book readable, intelligent and entertaining. This book will be of interest to the expert in the field, the student looking for a practical field approach and the inquisitive business leader.

—Dr. David Farrar, Managing Partner, Koliso.

Anthropology has ordinarily concerned itself with identifying particular habits of each culture it studied. In this effort we see a look across cultures at mythologies and business practices to find universal structures behind them-a critical perspective for a ethical global business leader who wants to be successful in the coming decade.

—Jim Hansen, former NASDAQ company CEO and Adjunct Professor

There is not one truth but only our perception of the truth. John Mirocha is an excellent observer. He added new perspectives and showed me, by simple real life stories, that every situation can be a learning situation.

—Martin Lammers, Director, Human Resources Management, Maastricht University

You have organized *Perspective* in a fashion that allows the reader to learn, understand, reflect and develop personal or organizational action steps regarding critical leadership and cultural change issues. Your book's structure that includes short stories, in-depth references and thought provoking questions will keep me busy as I continue to gain, "PERSPECTIVE" on myself and my company.

—Gary V. Lee, President & Chief Executive Officer, Rahr Corporation

To Linda, Erin, Jordan and to all my friends, colleagues, students and clients who provided the inspiration to conceptualize the book and many of the examples contained in the book. May you always see the world as a place to dream, live and learn.

CONTENTS

Introduction	1
1. The Context: Complexity and Uncertainty	7
2. Perspective	14
3. Anthropologists in Business?	23
4. Perspective, Leadership and Culture	57
5. Five Insights	72
5.1 Look Beneath the Surface	73
5.2 You Are a Part of the Cultural System You Are Participating In	97
5.3 Participant Observation	121
5.4 Theoretical Sampling	152
5.5 Focus on the Whole and on the Interrelationships	171
6. Metacognition: Focus, Personal Discipline and the Five Insights.	192
7. Conclusions	210

viii

Appendix	219
Notes	220
Subject Index	229
Name Index	232
About the Author	234

STORIES

Flat Tires	18
Leading and Uncertainty	51
Falling Leaves	68
Run as the City Awakens	90
Another Life Lesson: Lost Luggage	115
Accountants Go Native	145
The Ramp Guy	167
What it Takes to Build a Culture with a Strong Sense of Community	187
Roadmap	203
Old Town Market	212

Introduction

Managers and leaders today are faced with new types of dilemmas.

Change, complexity, competition and uncertainty are the stuff of their organizational lives. More businesses, for example, are operating in a global arena challenging traditional views of business scope, competition and speed. And, managers are increasing their travel distances as well as time away from home and office. Communication is exploding through the Internet and an assortment of hand held communication devices including the simple cell phone. The workforce is diversifying by ethnicity, gender, nationality, distance and age causing us to learn about generation x and y employees, Thai, Dutch, Russian, Somali, Chinese and Argentine customs and the new demands of managing virtual employees and contractors. Management spans of control now include more individuals and many more time zones. In addition, senior managers are setting higher and higher expectations in terms of future as well as current performance, speed and innovation. The bar that delineates success from failure has been raised significantly.

An Example

A colleague starts her Monday morning with a conference call at six a.m. so she can discuss important issues with her non-US direct reports in Sao Paulo, Brazil, Copenhagen, Denmark, Jakarta,

Indonesia and Melbourne, Australia. She does so with a mug of coffee in her home office while her two children and husband get ready for school and the office. While talking on the phone, she composes an e-mail on her computer to summarize the key elements of what is being said in the telephone conversation. At 8:00 a.m., she texts her secretary from her cell phone in her car to arrange a 5:00 p.m. meeting with a direct report to discuss a highly visible project that is late and over budget. And, at 8:30 a.m. she enters a staff meeting with her colleagues at corporate headquarters. Then she returns to her office where she finds sixty email messages, a full voice mailbox and several hand written messages left on her desk from employees who must see her. She glances at her to do list and sighs. Like many managers today she must struggle to find her true priorities or get swallowed up in the scope, complexity and speed of the demands she faces. She feels overwhelmed but is afraid to admit it because she fears that her feelings may be viewed as a sign of weakness by her peers and superiors. She craves perspective.

This book began as an attempt to help my graduate business students better understand culture and the importance of its study to business leaders. A very simple version appeared early in 2000 as a photocopied set of materials produced by the University of St. Thomas. In 2002, I produced the first book length manuscript through my corporation, John Mirocha & Associates, Inc. It has grown over the years in both concept and length. We are grateful to readers who have told us the earlier version of book gave them a new perspective to understand their organizations through and that this perspective made a difference at work as well as in their personal lives.

However, it is time for an official update. The external environment of organizations has been changing even more rapidly, raising the complexity and uncertainty of leadership decision making significantly. We provide a new picture of our emerging business and life realities with insights from the complexity sciences, further accentuating the importance of a new view.

How to Get the Most from This Book

Most management books are written to promote thinking and reflecting. This book is written to promote studying and experimenting in addition to thinking and reflecting to take full advantage of the concepts presented. Think of this book as a personal working guide. Work sequentially through the chapters. The ideas and exercises build upon and reinforce each other over time. Pause periodically, and go back and review earlier thoughts, ideas and exercises.

Introduction. The Introduction begins with a story of a person who is in a situation where she is overwhelmed by the speed and complexity of her business world. The story illustrates a universal dilemma faced by many business leaders today—the need for new tools and ideas to gain perspective.

Chapter 1, The Context: Complexity and Uncertainty uses the metaphor of a geographic map to explore our concepts of management. A map is a representation of a concept or a cluster of concepts that provide a vehicle for us to better understand something new. It is also used to plan and navigate one's course of action. The chapter raises the question of what is on our current business leadership map and if it needs to be updated given the changes in the world around us.

Chapter 2, Perspective defines the concept the book explores, perspective, paying special attention to why it is so important for business leaders today. Perspective is the ability to step outside of one's current situation and view it from a more objective and dispassionate point of view. Having a clearer and more accurate perspective allows one to view the situation one is in a new, more insightful way, seeing to the core of complex issues. A series of questions are posed to help the reader to better understand their perspective.

Chapter 3, Anthropologists in Business? provides the reader with a better understanding of what anthropological thinking is and why it is important to business leaders. Here, the three goals of the book are discussed: to increase leadership perspective, to increase self-understanding, and to improve business performance.

Chapter 4, Perspective, Leadership and Culture. This section of the book provides an introduction to cultural anthropology and its use in business. Complexity and uncertainty are discussed in some detail as they apply to the need for an increased perspective in business leadership and leadership development. The concept of culture is explored helping the reader understand better how it can be utilized by business people to gain insight into important, emergent and white water business applications.

Chapter 5, Five Insights. This section of the guide takes the reader through ideas and exercises that will help develop or improve leadership perspective.

- ***Look Beneath the Surface***. This chapter teaches the reader how to sharpen the skills of observation, patience and insight.
- ***You Are a Part of the Cultural System You are Studying*** offers the reader important ideas concerning seeing one's self as a functioning part of the world. Too often we see ourselves as outsiders to organizational dilemmas.
- ***Participant Observation*** describes some of the techniques that cultural anthropologists use to study culture and offers templates for the reader to use when conducting qualitative research.
- ***Theoretical Sampling.*** This chapter clarifies how our perceptions are controlled by what we pay attention to. It also provides exercises to help the reader broaden and sharpen skills for framing/viewing the world.
- ***Focus on the Whole and the Interrelationships*** summarizes and pulls together the key ideas from the other sections of the guide. A case study illustrating this principle is included. And it provides suggestions for more consciously using the insights and skills developed in the book to see and explore the *systemness* of the world.

Chapter 6, Meta-cognition: Focus, Personal Discipline and the Five Insights. *This chapter shows how to use the five insights as a dynamic learning and development system.*

Chapter 7, Conclusions. The last chapter helps the reader pull together his or her own insights regarding a personal leadership perspective and action plan.

This book is a practical aid in learning to view business dilemmas through the eyes of a cultural anthropologist without the abstract notions and jargon associated with a field of scientific inquiry that is more than one hundred years old. The ideas and exercises contained herein will help you build a *better perspective*. It will help you climb to a place where you have a clearer view of what is really going on in your industry or organization. You will be able to look past today's events and practices and see to the core of human and business processes. This book will also help you *to reflect and better understand yourself*, especially your biases and actions and how they influence your behavior and the behavior of others. Finally, this work will help you know if, when, where and how *to act to improve the business performance of your firm*. If you have an edgy trigger finger, you will learn a methodology of patience, observation and reflection to aim before you shoot. If you are more laissez-faire or caught up in the distractions provided by the complexity and speed of change, the exercises provided in this work will help you learn a discipline to help you discover the true opportunities and the need to act.

1.   *The Context: Complexity and Uncertainty*

I often talk about our personal view of the world as a personal map. A map guides us on our journey in business and life. This metaphor has been helpful to my students and clients. I have used various maps over the years to show how, over time, you can see your approximations of all things geographic. Very old European maps (1), for example, used by early world explorers, lack both big picture accuracy and accuracy in the details compared to today's maps which use sophisticated satellite images and mathematical formulas. Early maps were not much of a guide for explorers. Columbus thought he was going to India! We must remember and appreciate that maps are shaped and limited by the economic, social, technological and political realities of the day. A map, no matter how general or inaccurate, is still a map. It helps us plan and navigate. But it is the experience and learning of undertaking the voyage and experiencing the map's and our own navigational flaws that helps us update and improve our maps and thus our planning, navigation, experience and effectiveness.

A map can be a metaphor for our concepts of life and business. We have maps of the family, the political system, education, leisure and most things in life. These maps help us plan and navigate through the challenges we face. They also have an impact on our experience with the world that they attempt to approximate. If the map is inaccurate, it can cause problems.

Remember, a map is not just a map; it is a view of the world.

My views of our geographical, social and political world change frequently, which is not surprising given the world we live in. Connecting with your favorite news source instantaneously takes you around the world to unfolding events. A few years ago, for example, a friend showed me something called the Peters Projection Map (2) that got me thinking differently about the world I had experienced though my international business travel and the world I see on the television news. This map shows countries in proportion to their relative sizes. It is based upon German historian Arno Peters' decimal grid. I'd never really thought about the map's accuracy in my favorite atlas before. Now I could better see distances I had covered that seemed unusually long based on the atlas map and especially the 1950 map that hung on the gray, cement block wall in mom and dad's basement. The 1950 map showed a relatively small South America positioned almost directly below North America, a short distance away. A trip of eight and a half hours from Miami to San Paulo, Brazil now seemed about right after viewing Peters' map. And the four hour time change made sense as well. The atlas map is based on another mathematical formula and the maps are often cut off to fit a book page. And, the basement map included non-North American continents and nations merely as after thoughts.

Why a New World Map?

When viewing older maps (1, 3) it is clear that they were created with a bias toward the cartographer's nation's centrality and the separation and isolation of nations and peoples caused by sheer distance. U.S maps I had seen in elementary and high school also placed the US in the middle with lots of detail added such as capital cities, mountains and rivers. The further you got away from the U.S the less detail there was. These maps were made at a time that lacked the sophisticated cartographical technology that is available today. However, the lack of technology only explains a small part of the errors. Europe and America dominated the world economically, politically, socially and technologically. No wonder that America and Europe dominate the center of most maps in the West leaving other continents on the edge of the page.

We now stand at the dawning of an age characterized by a growing awareness of the interdependence of all nations and all peoples. The Peters map provides a helpful, corrective, lens to the distortions of traditional maps. While the map is superior in its portrayal of proportions and sizes, its importance goes far beyond questions of cartographic accuracy. It creates a new view of our world. In this complex and interdependent world, the peoples of the world deserve the most accurate portrayal of their world.

Mapping Change and Globalization

A few years ago, my geographic map of the world and the concept of global business was challenged and enriched as I studied a new book called The World is Flat, by Thomas Friedman (4). Mr. Friedman is a three time Pulitzer Prize winner for his work at the *New York Times,* where he serves as the foreign affairs columnist. He discusses the history of globalization and states, "But

Globalization 3.0 not only differs from the previous eras in how it is shrinking and flattening the world and in how it is empowering individuals. It is different in that Globalization 1.0 and 2.0 were driven primarily by European and American individuals and businesses. Globalization 3.0 is going to be more and more driven not only by individuals but also by much more diverse – non-Western, non-white—group of individuals. Individuals from every corner of the flat world are being empowered." This flattening is being driven by the internet, global outsourcing and supply chain activities and the growing wealth outside of Europe and America. (See the story, *Flat Tires*, page 13 of this book for more discussion of The World is Flat.) Friedman helped me see more clearly the collapsing of time and distance as mental constructs. In a flat world, they are minor considerations.

Of course, globalization is not a new thing, as author Nayan Chanda reminds us in his 2007 book, Bound Together: How Traders, Preachers, Adventurers, and Warriors Shaped Globalization (5). Since humans migrated from Africa approximately 200,000 years ago and dispersed throughout the world, we have found countless ways and reasons to push and test our physical, socio-cultural and intellectual boundaries, seeking resources, connections, relationships and growth in a natural, human process that defines us and illustrates our nature as human beings. While many human stories of globalization are laced with greed, cruelty and war, others are powerful stories of hope, growth and meaning. Whatever epoch we describe and analyze, we find that a more globally interdependent world is inevitable and needs to be better understood and perhaps, even embraced.

An analysis of maps reminds us that all constructs, whether a map, a menu or a social institution such as a business, is a contemporary construct. It is based on the cultural perceptions, needs and intellectual concepts prevalent at the time. It is only over time that we can look back and better see the assumptions that we made in their creation as biased and limited. Being better able to see our maps and assumptions in real time, rather than in retrospect, is important to us as we live our lives because we can see the traps inherent in these constructs and navigate our path more purposefully and efficiently as a result. As designers, perhaps we become a little smarter and do not succumb to the whims of contemporary society but look deeper for more fundamental principles to guide our institutions and lives as we experience the complexity and uncertainty of change on a global scale.

- Do the conceptual maps that you use to guide your personal and business activities need updating to better reflect the world we now live in? If so, how?

- Do those maps need to be tempered with a look toward a deeper and wiser understanding of life's issues and approaches so we do not get lost in the contemporary sea of change? If so, how?

Notes:
(1) For a map used by early explorers, see http://www.henry-davis.com/MAPS/LMwebpages/257.html.
(2) Peters, Arno. *Die Neue Kartographie/The New Cartography* (in German and English). Klagenfurt, Austria: Carinthia University; New York: Friendship Press, 1987.
(3) A good place to view a variety of maps is http://www.nationalgeographic.org/maps/.
(4) Friedman, Thomas. The World is Flat: A Brief History of the Twenty-First Century. Farrar, Straus and Giroux, 2006.
(5) Chanda, Nayan. Bound Together: How Traders, Peachers, Adventurers, and Warriors Shaped Globalization. Yale University Press, 2007.
(6) Einstein Albert. http://rescomp.stanford.edu/~cheshire/EinsteinQuotes.html.

"The significant problems we face cannot be solved at the same level of thinking we were at when we created them (6)."

Albert Einstein

2. *Perspective*

Perspective is the ability to step outside of one's current situation and view it from a more objective and dispassionate point of view. Perspective is based on understanding the maps one uses to perceive and navigate the world as well as the maps others use. Having a clearer and more accurate perspective allows one to view the situation one is in a new, more insightful way, seeing to the core of complex issues. The result is finding clear priorities and thoughtful, prudent solutions.

A lack of perspective can lead to poor personal and business performance. Unclear decision making criteria, looking at the wrong priorities or being dulled by the sheer speed and complexity of today's business and life situations are often at the root of not having an accurate perspective. Unwise choices build on each other creating problems that make things worse, not better. Using the wrong priorities wastes precious energy. Being dulled by complexity makes it difficult to find the key leverage points in an important business dilemma.

I used to know a business manager named Jack whose story illustrates a perspective paradox and its personal and organizational consequences. For years and years he worked for a strong, authoritarian executive named Sam who had significant influence in the corporation. Jack was Sam's technician, gopher, problem solver, detail person and loyal follower. When Sam retired, he made sure that Jack was promoted to director and put in charge of the department. This was not a very wise decision as the company was growing quickly needing a broader range of services from Jack's department and Jack was unable to respond to the new challenges. The department started to flounder because of the leadership vacuum left by Sam and the department's inability to meet the needs of their internal customers. Then, several of Jack's direct reports began initiating their own agendas as the department's mission in order to move things ahead. They also attempted to build coalitions of employees to support them. Over the course of a year the department neared chaos. The coalitions were competing for power within the leadership vacuum. Jack hardly noticed as he buried himself in budgets and administrative minutia. The corporation's senior managers became aware of the issues and Jack's department was put under the leadership of Peter. In addition, a management coach was enlisted to help Jack and his department build a common vision and mission and the supporting work process that would make it productive once again. Peter told Jack that his job depended on his ability to rise above the administrative tasks he had performed for Sam and become a true leader of the department. Jack's coach, after lengthy discussions with Peter, other senior managers and Jack's staff, told him the same thing. Next, Jack and his coach developed a personal game plan for Jack to develop the skills and perspective he needed to succeed. Jack started to respond to the fear of losing his job and the aid of a supportive and professional coach. However, every time there was even the smallest potential crisis, Jack would call Sam for advice. The advice seemed to paralyze him in the face of the challenge. In a reactive mode, Jack would go back to his old ways. The coach and Peter saw this pattern emerge repeatedly over the course of six months. They shared their observations with Jack in the hope of pushing him out of the problematic pattern. When this didn't work, they threatened him with losing his job if the pattern was not broken. A few months later, Jack was demoted and a manager from a related area added Jack's department to his domain. Jack took early retirement a few months later.

Jack's story illustrates that sometimes even capable managers can get caught in conceptual and behavioral patterns that are extremely difficult to break. In this case, Jack was caught between the old world his boss created of control and repetition and the emerging world that was characterized more by the need to change and adapt to the growth of the company and the emerging needs of his department's internal customers. The inability to recognize the dysfunctional cycle and consciously grow beyond it led to poor, ineffective problem solving

> *"Change is inevitable.*
> *Growth is optional."*
>
> Vicki

and decision-making. It caused Jack to lose his job and it put his department in jeopardy for three years. He also lost four employees who couldn't live in the politically charged leadership vacuum that was created and thus left for opportunities at other companies. The tell tale sign of lack of perspective is when an individual or entire leadership team attempts to use old, ineffectual ways to solve emerging issues. In the face of these emerging issues, they work the old ways harder and harder to little or no avail, exacerbating an already critical situation.

Gaining and maintaining perspective is a journey. It involves a conscious learning and unlearning process and taking stock of the important events and life challenges we face. It is better to take steps to ensure that you have perspective because once it is lost it is difficult to regain. Take a moment to answer the following questions to take stock of your current situation.

1. What are the key drivers of business change for your industry and business?

   a. Which drivers of change are likely to be predictable? Why?

   b. Which drivers of change are likely to be unpredictable? Why?

2. What *new* challenges and demands are these drivers creating for you?

3. What concepts, skills and processes do you usually use to solve problems and make decisions?

4. What new premises, skills and behaviors will you and your business need to lead in this emerging environment?

5. Are you open to change? How much change?

Flat Tires

Columbus reported to his king and queen that the world was round and he went down in history as the man who first made this discovery. I returned home and shared my discovery only with my wife, and only in a whisper. Honey, I confided, I think the world is flat.

Thomas Friedman

The phone always rings at the wrong time. And it usually isn't who you want it to be. As a guy who works from a home office, I know this well. I frequently drop something important I am working on to pick up the phone to get a telemarketer's call. I have learned to let it ring so I can complete my thought, proposal or comments on a student's assignment. I let the phone ring quite a bit this afternoon as I was buried under a snow drift of student papers. I was engrossed in reading them as the first of a forecast of nine inches of snow was starting to accumulate outside my office window.

I picked up the phone to check for messages while doing the initial prep work for dinner, thirty minutes later. I had only one new message. I smiled and felt proud to have missed five calls that didn't leave a message, probably all telemarketers. Then, as I listened to the one new message, my mood changed. It was from my daughter Erin who had not one but two flat tires and was stranded in a dark parking lot twenty miles across town.

I called her cell phone immediately. Erin was telling me her situation when my wife, Linda, asked that I hand her the phone. After she determined that Erin was fine, she said we had free towing service associated with one of our credit cards. She told Erin she would call and get the tow truck ordered. Linda wrote the street intersection on a sheet of paper and said she would call her back in a couple minutes to confirm that the tow truck was on the way.

As Linda called the 1-800 number, I got back to preparing dinner. As I diced an onion, I overheard her state, "The car is at the intersection of Lone Oak Road and Pilot Knob Road," twice. Then she spelled L-O-N-E O-A-K twice very slowly and articulately. She put her hand over the phone and said to me, "This person isn't familiar with the area and there is a slight time gap when we speak to each other. I wonder if I am talking to someone internationally at a call center." Then she said, "Thank you," to the person on the other end of the phone, turned to me and said, "He will set the thing up and call us back in a few minutes." We looked at each other as parents. Parents can conjure up all kinds of dark scenarios at a time like this when everything isn't clear, certain or in control and their children are involved.

Just as my stock started to simmer a few minutes later, the phone rang. I said to Linda, "Ask him where he is?" thinking less as a father and more as a professor of a course with the term global in its title. Linda answered the phone. It was indeed our tow truck getter. He said that Dick's Towing would be there in forty-five to sixty minutes. He also gave us the driver's name and his cell phone number. Then I heard Linda ask, "Can you tell me where you are?" She smiled, and said, "Thank you," as she hung up. She turned to me, smiled and said, "He is in Bangalore, India and his name is Vijay."

I consider myself a world citizen. I have traveled extensively internationally. And, Linda coordinates a college Learning Center which employs and caters to students who speak as a group a total of 85 languages. However, all the rational ideas about globalization go out the window when the safety of your daughter is in the hands of someone you don't know who is working the graveyard shift twelve thousand miles away.

The tow truck arrived about an hour later, deposited the car at the service station and dropped my daughter off at her apartment, just as we sat down for our dinner.

Globalization is a phenomenon that is in the news daily. Some of us see it as a simple issue that we should either be for or against. However, it is neither simple nor something that you can be for or against, as it is affecting our lives every day whether we want it to or not in ways that many of us don't seem to notice. Thomas Friedman, author of The World is Flat (4), tells us that there have been two waves of globalization. Globalization 1.0 encompassed a time when the old world and the new world were linked and integrated through trade. The second era of globalization, Globalization 2.0, was driven by multi-national organizations. Eras one and two shrunk the world and integrated it. The third era, Globalization 3.0, has just begun. It, Friedman says, "is going to be more and more driven not only by individuals but also by a much more diverse – non-Western, non-white – groups of individuals." Globalization 3.0 is being fueled by rising standards of living in developing countries, outsourcing, the internet and the continuing push of Globalization 1.0 and 2.0. The shift in power that may come with Globalization 3.0 will be interesting to think more about and notice as we do our daily activities.

I think fondly of Vijay, the guy twelve thousand miles way, who very competently contacted Dick's Towing, twenty-five miles away, got the tow truck there successfully, and gave us the tow truck driver's name and cell phone number that provided for us, in turn, a little sense of security in today's uncertain, global world. He taught me an important lesson. The world isn't round anymore.

Epilogue. As I have reflected on this experience and written this story, I have asked myself why the flat tire experience resonated with me to the degree it did. We have talked to call centers around the US and internationally about credit card expenditures, computer viruses and the like. However, we haven't outsourced anything as near and dear to us as our daughter's safety before. And, I have realized that I am guilty of a bias that comes with an old, large world concept that I will introduce as *distance bias*. Distance bias is a preference for people closer to home and familiarity solving problems and making key decisions for you. It is a bias because in a flat world, linked by technology, distance doesn't matter.

Lessons Learned:

1. The personal "maps" we use to navigate our lives need significant change given globalization.
2. When issues are personalized and emotional they become more meaningful.
3. In a shrinking world, we must be aware of distance bias.
4. It's a good idea to have a towing service when you need it.

3. _Anthropologists in Business?_

A flight from Miami to San Paulo glides over the Amazon. A business passenger from the U.S. gazes out his window at the Rain Forest below. The scenery is lush green, punctuated by a few morning clouds and puffs of smoke. Over the past few weeks, in preparation for his trip, he started to pay attention to articles in newspapers and magazines about Brazil. He learned that beneath the canopy of trees he was now looking at waged a controversy of enormous proportions. The area, rich in natural resources, is being burned systematically by ranchers and farmers. In 1997 alone, 7,800 acres of rain forest was burned. The rate of burning is not slowing, even today. Now, a little more than a decade later, some experts state that the tipping point for deforestation in the Amazon is twenty percent of the land, a number we are approaching quickly. This is a crisis point of possible ecological disaster, because deforestation does not act in a linear fashion. It is a system that behaves in a synergistically destructive way compounded by climate change, further deforestation and fire (1).

The rain forest is prized by environmentalists and medical and pharmacological researchers as one of the last pristine rain forests in the world; it is home to the world's largest collection of animal and plant species, as well as troves of bacteria and fungi whose medicinal and nutritional values have yet to be studied. The Amazon is also the home of 5,000 indigenous people belonging to seventeen tribes including the Tukano and Yanomami, considered to be a few of the last Stone Age tribes in existence. Industrialists, environmentalists, tribal leaders and government officials have conflicting priorities for the future of this area and its people. He wonders how they will ever work it out.

The business person is on his way to a meeting. He is a representative from one of two merging firms who is on a cultural integration team. Individuals from both companies have formed the team, which will meet to discuss issues of common values, technology, business systems, product and service compatibility and potential layoffs. There are companies like these in many industries that are consolidating to seek economies of scale, take a step toward becoming global or to add key competencies. The business person visualizes the meetings ahead in an attempt to get the issues outlined through the mental fog of his overnight flight. While his company has grown steadily through acquisition, the acquired company has been family held. What will that mean? He has never been to Brazil before and is concerned about language and culture issues. He also fears that he may uncover different assumptions and values regarding the Brazilian company's vision and mission versus those of his own company. He realizes that he feels apprehensive about the meetings as he is stepping into issues he hasn't quite faced before. He asks the flight attendant for coffee to help him become more alert. He opens a noted, international business publication and begins to page through it. A blind job advertisement catches his eye.

Seeking cultural anthropologists with demonstrated skills in brokering and resolving strategic, cross cultural business issues, especially where economic, technological and human issues are intertwined.

He wonders, "What company is this? Why would they seek the assistance of anthropologists? What is it exactly that anthropologists do? How can they help?" He closes his eyes and falls back to sleep in a swirl of thoughts about rain forests, complex business issues and anthropologists.

Technician to Management Transition

Many managers like the person above or Jack (pages 10-11) are promoted into their managerial jobs because they excel at technical work, the ability to perform specific, routine and repetitive tasks and to solve problems and find solutions that work within the current business model. The job of management, however, takes more than doing repetitive work and solving technical problems. Managerial work is not doing just individual problem solving. It is getting work done through others. This step above the day-to-day issues increases the scope of the job, adds abstraction and the need to conceptualize about more complex issues and requires a perspective that is more strategic. It also involves more complex human interaction. To become a manager, an individual must have the intention to manage and the strategic, human and administrative skills to drive performance through the technical work and problem solving of others enabled by a consciously developed, meaningful and engaging organizational culture. Our airline passenger above (unlike Jack), is starting to think about the issues he faces which will require him to enlarge his perspective dramatically to make a contribution to his company. He seems to be forming managerial intent.

Many individuals suffer and fail to make the transition from technician to manager. Some can't think beyond the technical aspects of the job and the simple problem solving they do every day. Others can't grow outside of their current job identity to consider the purpose of management, much less the future. Still others have poor human relations skills. Those who fail in the transition to management do so because their job perspective and skills are too limited for them to succeed given the challenges they face. They fail because they don't learn from the leadership crucibles they encounter (2). But it isn't entirely their fault. We need to look at the larger cultural system surrounding such managers. We need to look at the expectations and perspectives of those who are promoting the Jacks into management. We must examine their beliefs, values and overall perspectives as well. How does the promoting manager view the business and the organization? If promoting manager views the business and organization as one large machine, the idea is that the machine is working, but from time to time a part needs to be replaced. Little or no creative, innovative or strategic thought is required of that new part. And, considering an improved part with different functionality is out of the question as it would cause friction with the other parts and the mechanical system. Sam's replacement, in this view, should be Sam 2.0; Jack. Thus, Jack would be a good fit for Sam's job as he had most of the functionality. However, new challenges were emerging and the part (or Jack) could no longer

"The world in which the executive lives, works, and thinks is now and always will be an inherently uncertain and irrational one, in which the shortest distance between two points is seldom a straight line. In such a world, tools based on the false realities of management science, past experience, or market intelligence can be at best crutches and at worst deceiving mirages of truth in a desert of imperfect predictability. Tools of humanity, intuition, emotion, and sentiment offer the only real hope for survival in the long run (3)."

Suresh Srivasta and Associates

perform the tasks necessary for change and success. The part was static and it needed to be more dynamic and capable of growth.

Maybe this mechanical, machine metaphor worked a long time ago but not today. The metaphor for the organization today needs to be more organic than mechanical as new challenges face the organization that require more than simple problem solving techniques. Managers today need to develop more adaptable, imaginative, robust, and innovative premises to charter a new course in an emerging world. In addition, today's employees are not machine parts. They are individuals with their own aspirations for work, career and community and seek engagement and meaning in their work and with their employers. Finally, administrative and managerial tasks are often more challenging today given the need to manage employee performance, manage a budget and work with customer needs and expectations and increased competition on a larger scale in an information intensive, warp-speed environment. Like endangered species that do not have the skills to cope with a changing environment, some employees and would-be managers lack the adaptability to respond to their environment. Their future is endangered.

Management to Leadership Transition

Managing today's employees has become an oxymoron as we now think more about leading, which implies strategic work in addition to the management of those activities that are more mundane but none-the-less important.

Moving from management to leadership includes mastering significant challenges. It includes managing the larger scope, complexity and uncertainty of the strategic issues that leaders face. It means creating tomorrow's successful organization while managing the tension between getting the day-to-day work done successfully while creating the future. Another significant job for executives is talent development; creating a pipeline of future managers and leaders. And, finally, leaders are responsible for bottom line results both short term and long term. Leadership is about growth, development and change, while management is about perfecting the current business model. Leadership, according to management author Peter Vaill (4), is more performing art than science. Effective leadership requires responding creatively and constructively to the challenges leaders face. This differentiates leaders who are successful from those who are not.

We must determine the important transitions in the career of an employee from individual contributor/technician to supervisor to functional manager, from functional manager to general manager and from manager to leader. This process has been researched and described by noted authors initially in the 1980's such as Morgan W. McCall, Michael M. Lombardo, and Ann M. Morrison (5), then by Noel Tichy (6), Morgan McCall, Jr. (7, 8) and by Ram Charan, Stephen Drotter and James Noel (9) and most recently in an excellent selection of articles on executive leadership development, Kerry Bunker, et al's Extraordinary Leadership: Addressing the Gaps in Senior Executive Development (10). The message is clear. Organizations of all sizes in all industries face a competitive war for talent. Being able to attract, recruit, develop and retain talent, especially leadership talent, is a competitive advantage. Creating a leadership pipeline of talent requires top management direction and support as well as organizational processes to drive the system and culture that nurtures it. Leadership development is not relegated only to the HR department. It is one of the cornerstones of effective executive leadership.

1. Is your view of your business world that of a technician, manager or leader?

2. What does your company do to fill its leadership pipeline with talent to meet today's and tomorrow's challenges?

3. What developmental need should you address to fulfill your career aspirations?

4. Does the culture of your organization assist or impede the development of leaders?

Complexity, Uncertainty and Business Leadership

Too often business people have wanted their insights quick, cheap and simple, which is a recipe for disaster given today's complexity and uncertainty. Simple, quick solutions put Band Aids on dilemmas rather than solving them. The Band Aid hides the problem for a while masking it from sight as the problem continues to grow. What is needed is a more ecological view; a view which encompasses a broader scope of issues and the curiosity and discipline to look both at the parts and their interdependencies in a moving landscape.

A new approach to understanding the realities underneath the aforementioned issues as well as technologies to better grasp their significance have been developed over the past decade for the general public. Concepts such as adaptation, morphogenesis and disequilibrium theory have been available for a long time but sequestered in academe in departments of anthropology, biology, zoology and other life sciences. Many of these discoveries, both old and new, began in the physical and social sciences giving birth today to something called the "new sciences." These "new sciences" included chaos theory, complex adaptive systems, non-linear dynamics and quantum theory. A variety of authors have taken these ideas and applied them to the field of organizational theory and management such as Senge (11), Wheatley (12), Pascale, Millemann and Gioja (13), Olson and Eoyang (14) and Stacey (15). What these authors are suggesting is that our business world, in many respects, has become more complex and uncertain and it is becoming more difficult for leaders to decipher the emerging challenges, much less reach agreement on both strategic and tactical matters. And, their leadership approach needs to adapt to their changing surroundings and challenges. Ron Heifitz, the Directior of the Leadership Education Project at the John F. Kennedy School of Government, Harvard University, makes a distinction between the world of technical leadership and adaptive leadership (16, 17). In the technical realm, authority provides problem definition and solution, authority protects the organization from an external threat and authority restores order and maintains the organization's norms. In the adaptive realm, new types of complexity are fraught with increasing uncertainty and lack of agreement. In this world, Heifitz says that leadership is a razor's edge because one has to oversee a sustained period of social disequilibrium during which employees confront the contradictions of the current state and the needs for a new path. Leaders must use authority differently than in the technical state where they provide answers. In the adaptive state, leaders use their authority to identify the adaptive challenge and produce questions about problem definitions and solutions. Authority also discloses the external threat, exposes conflicts or lets them emerge, and authority challenges norms and nurtures new norms that need to be identified and adapted for organizational survival (15, pg. 126). And, most importantly, the leader uses authority to orchestrate the discussion which leads to new strategies and tactics rather than to provide those solutions him or herself. For, in the adaptive world, the leader does not always know the answer. Therefore the leader's role must change to more of an orchestrator of processes that engage a broader community of leaders in the discussion of the emerging challenges. Of course, wise leaders know that people are more likely to support a change that they have helped develop. This change of role from technical problem solver manager to leader is a difficult one. The transition to leadership requires the leader to use authority sparingly and to rely on others to help research strategic issues, discuss them and propose courses of action.

To better understand this way of thinking, I have included some of the attributes of a model proposed by Ralph Stacey (15) to better clarify the movements of a firm when exposed to emerging threats. In example one, I will emphasize the dilemmas facing the firm's leaders over the past thirty years more than their actual decisions. In the second example, I will emphasize the internal leadership challenges and ensuing decisions made by firm leaders in what Vaill calls whitewater.

Emergent Issues and Leadership Responses

Table 3.1: Three Situations (see next page) describes three different environments and types of issues that businesses must understand and address successfully to survive and grow. First, there are simple, technical issues, where there is little uncertainty and much agreement on a course of activities to ensure growth and profitability. These matters are considered mechanistic issues and their solutions are based in simple problem-solving techniques. The authors also suggest that this view of the world is a mechanistic or Newtonian view where present systems are well defined, change is slow and small, interdependencies are simple, certainty is high and turbulence is low. Solutions to these issues have been rational, top down, expert driven and use classical planning mechanisms. Businesses often are full of process guides, spec sheets and error reduction practices to solve problems and generate solutions to these issues.

Second, organizations face emerging situations where new forms of competition or changing world events alter the competitive

Table 3.1. Three Situations

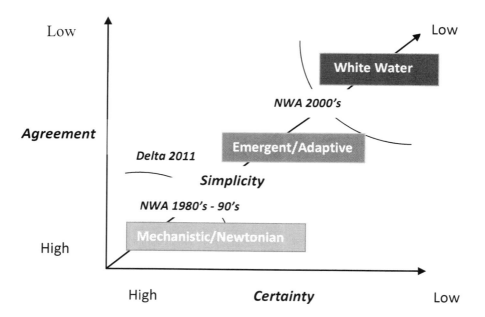

landscape. The challenge for leadership is to adapt to the changing landscape which is defined by the emergent properties. Let us use the example of North West Airlines (now Delta) over the last 30 years to illustrate the sheer number, magnitude and intensity of emerging issues they have had to identify and respond to. (See Appendix 1. NWA/Delta Timeline.)

The world has changed significantly over the past 30 years for the airline industry and Delta. Beginning with the merger of NWA and Republic Airlines (1986), a period of relative stability and growth occurred leading to a time of mechanistic issues to perfect and extend the model for business success at the time. These issues included safety, hub and spoke route efficiencies, union - labor issues and growth. Then in the 1990's things started to shift competitively due to emerging issues around the world. While we can only imagine the challenges senior managers faced and the reasons for the actions they took, those of us who traveled on the airline frequently, lived in Minneapolis and read the daily newspaper, can venture a good guess as to their situation. The mechanistic world of the 1980's was now characterized by competition for their routes from traditional providers as well as regional carriers, high employee salaries and significant, acrimonious labor relations, a growing and profitable business clientele, increased international routes, passengers and profit and stable fuel costs. However, their fleet was aging and their fuel consumption was very high.

A new, more uncertain and complex world emerged beginning in the 1990's with non-traditional entrants such as Southwest

35

Airlines and Jet Blue building a new business model that is based on low costs fares, a non-union workforce and a no frill, yet better customer service. (See Table 1, NWA 2000's.) It took several years for the so-called legacy carriers to recognize that the playing field had changed. They spent most of the nineties and the first few years of the millennium cutting costs to maintain their competitiveness. Then, their attention was captivated by the events of 911 and the resulting reduction of domestic air travel. They were also challenged by a rash of other events and emerging issues including increasing fuel costs, the bird flu outbreak, a recession and war. Throughout this tumultuous time, NWA drove its costs down, upgraded its fleet, changed its unionized structure and defended its hub and spoke system. They also alienated many of their loyal customers in the process. But, in the end, this was not enough. They needed a partner, Delta, to survive.

They were acquired by Delta in 2008, building the largest airline in the world. However, even after the post-merger integration of systems, routes, fleet, crews, policies, and culture, Delta and other carriers continue to need to adapt to rollercoaster fuel costs, competition, international political and economic events and the reemergence of an old competitor, the railroad.

The events that have challenged Delta can be considered an emergent situation. Traditional business forms and practices were no longer capable of sustaining the airline. These emergent situations needed strategies that recognized that current practices were threatening their survival, change was fast and unpredictable, interdependencies were more complex, certainty was low and turbulence was high. By sticking to their platform of low cost, non-unionized labor, marginal service and major hubs in cities like in the Twin Cities and Detroit, they survived. Jad Mouawad, in a May 2011 New York Times article, summarizes this history by saying,

Financially, the merger provided a big boost to Delta's bottom line. Delta posted its highest profit in a decade last year. But even as the integration into a single carrier was hitting its stride, Delta's operations struggled. The airline had the worst record among large carriers for on-time arrivals last year, and it accounted for a third of all customer complaints, the worst of any airline, for categories like service and lost bags, according to the Transportation Department (18).

In March of 2009, I was on a NWA/Delta return flight from Denver to Minneapolis, where NWA's headquarters were prior to the merger. Just before landing, the lead flight attendant proudly announced that as of the next day, she and all other former NWA flight attendants would switch their attire to the Delta standard completing the integration of the two flight attendant workforces. The majority of passengers booed, laughed and jeered voicing their displeasure, not with just the change of attire which was mostly symbolic, but with the whole merger, and moving the corporate center to Atlanta under Delta's name.

The notion of emergent situations has been described historically in the life science literature as well as in the contemporary business literature. These emergent situations are governed,

Pascale, et al, suggest (13, pg. 12), by four principles:

1. Equilibrium is a precursor to death. When a living system is in a state of equilibrium, it is less responsive to change occurring around it. This places it at maximum risk.
2. In the face of threat, or even when galvanized by a compelling opportunity, living things move toward the edge of chaos. This condition evokes higher levels of mutation and experimentation, and fresh new solutions are more likely to be found.
3. When this excitation takes place, the components of the living system self-organize and new forms and repertoires emerge from the turmoil.
4. Living systems cannot be directed along a linear path. Unforeseen consequences are inevitable. The challenge is to disturb them in a manner that approximates the desired outcome.

The role of the leader is to recognize these emergent situations. Once recognized, the leader must use the appropriate techniques to address the issues. These are not simple, formula-based, management techniques. As principle four states above, the leader's role is to nudge the system along toward an end that approximates the desired outcome or vision. If these principles are properly employed, state the authors, allow business enterprises to thrive and revitalize themselves. In contrast, the machine age principles, when applied to emerging situations, although familiar and enduring, often quietly facilitate the stagnation and decline of the firm that is faced with discontinuous change. NWA, in retrospect, seems to have had a platform of decisions and practices that got them through their most important emergent challenges. They seemed to have recognized that equilibrium was a potential death spiral. They moved toward the edge of chaos both in Wall Street terms and customer satisfaction terms but managed to avoid failure. The bottom line was survival. By merging with another airline, it consolidated operations, improved efficiencies and got to a lower, overall cost position in an industry that is still predominantly cost driven. However, they have alienated many of their customers in the process. NWA/Delta has emerged from the chaos as a new entity but with significant issues on the horizon. It seems that the emergent issues, while significant, did not completely change the rules of the airline industry. They required NWA to go to its core to survive. NWA did not need to change it essence as a low cost provider to survive. But it could not make it on its own. NWA needed the size and resulting efficiencies of scale with Delta to survive.

A Business in Whitewater

A third situation type has been characterized by Peter Vaill, in his book <u>Managing as Performing Art</u>. He states,

Today's leaders and managers are in the position of stepping into the dark with most of the initiatives they propose. When you step into the dark, you still make the assumption that your foot is going to come down on something solid, even if you don't know it is going to be. Today's executive can't even make that assumption.

This metaphor clearly… vividly conveys a sense of energy and movement. Things are only partially under control, yet the effective navigator of the rapids is not behaving randomly or aimlessly. Intelligence, experience, and skill are being exercised, albeit in ways that we hardly know how to perceive, let alone describe (4, pg. 3).

Vaill is the person who coined the term *whitewater* as an emergent business situation. Whitewater is the most transformational type of challenge that a business faces. It requires fundamental changes in form and substance to occur for survival to be realized. What is the role of the leader in whitewater? Two other metaphors used by academics, consultants and practitioners to describe the leader's role in times of high uncertainty, high complexity and low agreement are that of the improvisational jazz group and the improvisational comedian. The jazz group switches the roles of leader, follower and accompanist around a common theme or chord progression and the improvisational comedian juxtaposes comedic elements together to come up with new insights and humor in a spontaneous way.

> *"If you always do what you have always done, you will always get what you have always got."*
>
> Larry Wilson

A number of years ago I worked for a company that had grown steadily for more than 100 years. Sourcing and handling commodities from domestic and international markets was the basis of their business. These commodities had served the young company well as it made money from wise trades, storage, handling and transportation. Senior executives got their start in these businesses and commodity trading work became the central business model and skill set for employees to learn. As the company grew, however, commodities were worth less in their original state than if they were processed into goods that had more value for their customers and higher margins for the corporation's businesses. These new, emerging businesses were further up the vertical business hierarchy (vertical integration). The newer businesses became much more profitable than the historical commodity business. However, no one seemed to notice. The commodity business eventually hit a crisis point where their revenues barely met their expenses in the good years and didn't in the bad years. They needed to rethink their strategy and reinvent themselves as a business.

They had managed through the years with a mechanistic mentality and business model while the globalization of markets, the growing consumer foods movement and competitors generated emergent dilemmas for them to deal with. Unfortunately, their issues were buried within the revenue and cost stream of a very large company. When they hit whitewater, they didn't realize it at first as corporate leadership of the parent company, while holding them accountable for their business results like every other business unit, cut them some corporate slack as they understood the value they delivered as an entity and they cherished the experience they had running those businesses. Eventually, holding them accountable for their profitability as a standalone business won out over providing space for them to exist as an "unproductive" entity. To meet the demand of corporate leaders, they cut cost, reduced headcount, collapsed regions and fought a fight that they couldn't win, using solutions that mostly addressed the emergent issues with strategies that worked in the past. These strategies didn't address the fundamental change in the volatile, competitive, global marketplace or their evolving, and important role, in the larger business.

After more than a year of thinking and analysis, the combined business leadership of the commodity business and the parent corporation decided not to evaluate the business as a revenue generator but more as a cost center supporting other businesses with its work products and services. This decision shook many of the leaders of the commodity business and the greater corporation to their core. They all had begun their careers in this business unit and learned, what was considered at that time, the core skills needed to be successful in any of the corporation's up stream business units. Many of the leaders at that time believed that an employee needed to have had one of those jobs to use as a rung on the ladder which lead to senior management. They wondered how and if future leaders could learn the core skills of the business and climb the corporate ladder from a cost center versus the historically based robust engine of the company's profitability and growth. And, if trading commodities was no longer the chief engine of company profitability and growth, what was?

With the commodity business president Pete, I designed and facilitated the conference where the decision was announced to managers to move from a profit center business model to a cost center business model. The management team anguished through the issues at the retreat and reluctantly decided that it was best to move on and emphasize the growth of the bigger entity: the corporation. Once this agreement was reached, I asked each person to write on one sheet of paper what their hopes were and on another what they would have to let go of for the change to be productive. We discussed both the hopes and letting go ideas as a large group. Then, I collected the letting go papers and asked everyone to walk to the parking lot with me. I handed the sheets to the president who read a few out loud and then read his to the group as a whole. The group self-formed into a circle around the president who put the papers in a waste basket. Pete asked for a moment of silence and lit the papers on fire. Pete shared some important memories of his experience with the commodities business and said, "Good Bye."After a few minutes, the flames settled down and the smoke released its energy into the air. Individuals walked back into the meeting room where we focused the conversation on what the new vision, mission and values should be for the future business. There was nary a dry eye in this group of embattled managers. I later collected the ashes, put them into a small bottle, and delivered them to the business president a few days later with a label that said, "The Global Commodity Business: 1865-2006." It remained on his desk as a memento from an earlier time and a conversation starter for as long as I knew him. The beginning of the transformation process was symbolized by the urn and ashes of the old business and the new vision, mission and values statement that hung on the wall behind his desk.

The quick fix, mechanical mentality addressing complex issues with simplistic answers, seems to be changing. A realization is sweeping across the minds of managers around the world as they face situations like those outlined above. They realize that their years of business school training and business experience leave them wanting for an additional set of skills—skills to manage the new, complex world of explosive change and international commerce. And, they know simple solutions from the past—quick fixes—won't do. The wisdom of cultural anthropology provides a necessary perspective to explore and integrate these new views. Some companies are ahead of the curve, as the job advertisement for cultural anthropologists example demonstrates.

The Leader's New Role

The role of the leader must change as a company addresses emerging issues and whitewater. The leader no longer knows all of the answers. To provide leadership, the leader cannot deliver edicts and command like in the mechanical world with its known issues and proven solutions. In the emergent world, and even more so in whitewater, the leader becomes a facilitator of change creating forums for discussion. The leader provides platforms for debate and the articulation of scenarios for the future. She uses these forums to clarify the emergent or whitewater issues and to accelerate the creative thinking, innovation and problem solving that the situation calls for. The tools that the leader uses in emergent and white water situations are not simple process identification tools. The leader's tools include learning forums, scenario planning, story boarding and deep dives (19).

Ron Heifitz, in his <u>Leadership Without Easy Answers</u>, calls this leadership action *going to the balcony*. The leader must name the emerging issues, orchestrate a dialogue around the issues and move to a place where he can observe and direct the process. Why does the leader go to the balcony? For perspective! The balcony is a metaphor for leading as coordinating, nurturing and stewarding important thinking.

Leadership is both active and reflective. One has to alternate between participating and observing.... Rather than maintain perspective on the events that surround and involve us, we often get swept up by them. Consider the experience of dancing on a dance floor in contrast with standing on a balcony and watching other people dance. Engaged in the dance, it is nearly impossible to get a sense of the patterns made by everyone on the floor. Motion makes observation difficult... To discern the larger patterns on the dance floor – to see who is dancing with whom, in what groups, in what location, and who is sitting out which kind of dance – we have to stop moving and get to the balcony (16, pp. 252-253).

Anthropologists and other life scientists have studied competition, adaptation and survival for quite some time. Their focus has mostly been non-business situations. However, many of the dynamics that face cultures or societies in danger mirror the characteristics and dynamics of businesses in jeopardy. Leaders, whether tribal, governmental or corporate face the following leadership demands in times of emergent and whitewater realities. In order to be successful, they must:

1. Identify the trends and competitive pressures that create strategic issues for the company as it looks to the future. Leaders need to emphasize external realities especially to get the attention of a complacent company or one in denial.

2. Identify the adaptive challenges where people in the organization are conflicted over values or strategy. What questions must be asked to move the organization into complexity and uncertainty? What is the forum for discussing and addressing the questions and their implications best?

3. Regulate distress that is generated by the disequilibrium and the adaptive challenge. The emergent issues must be contained within limits that challenge the status quo but do not overwhelm key constituencies of the change.

4. Provide a forum which attempts to clarify authority, shared purposes, common identifications and other bonds of community to keep the organization together and provide a platform for discussion, debate and problem-solving.

5. Direct disciplined attention to the issues. Companies often

try to restore equilibrium by using old solutions to new problems or by reducing the overt manifestations of their internal tensions. The leader must take the organization to the edge of chaos to find solutions.

6. Mobilize the organization by giving them a stake and a voice in what needs to happen. In times of emergence and whitewater leaders do not necessarily have all of the answers. They must move to the balcony and become more of a facilitator and steward of the change process as key ideas for change emerge and decisions need to be considered and made.

7. Increase their ability to reflect on these important matters and to adapt themselves to changing business and leadership realities without getting burned out. They do this by getting to the balcony as needed to maintain and enrich their perspective. Heifitz (16, pg. 15) calls this *Taking the Heat*.

In summary, managers face dilemmas like no other time in history. To develop into leaders, they must come to terms with three important issues. First, they need to control their technical needs and identity and develop the intention to lead. Second, they must face the daunting complexity, uncertainty and scope of their new realm. As they do this, they need to understand that they do not necessarily know the answers and they must be able to articulate this and at the same time prepare a process to define emerging issues, develop alternatives and reach consensus on strategies and actions with their team. Third, they must seek perspective. They can find this perspective by seeking a place where they are apart from yet connected to the process they have developed and are orchestrating. However, the balcony is something more than a physical place; it is a frame of mind and a set of skills. It is the art and practice of perspective.

How does one develop and maintain perspective during times of dramatic change?

Notes:

(1) For rainforest facts go to http://www.discoverychannel.co.in/earth/fire/rainforest_fires /index.shtml or see, Report of the World Commission on Forests and Sustainable Development. Our Forests. Cambridge University, Press, 1999. and Ajl, Max. "Deforestation Pushing Amazon to Its Ecological Limits." Solve Climate News , February 23, 2010, , http://solveclimatenews.com/news/20100223/deforestation-pushing-amazon-its-ecological-limits.

(2) Bennis, Warren and R. Thomas. "Crucibles of Leadership." Harvard Business Review, 80, (9), 39, 2002.

(3) Srivasta, Suresh and Associates (Editors). The Executive Mind. Jossey-Bass, 1983, pg. 300.

(4) Vaill, Peter. Managing as Performing Art. Jossey-Bass, 1989.

(5) McCall, Morgan W., Michael M. Lombardo, and Ann M. Morrison. Lessons of Experience: How Successful Executives Develop on the Job. Lexington Books, 1988.

(6) Tichy, Noel. The Leadership Engine: How Winning Companies Build Leaders at Every Level. HarperBusiness, 1997.

(7) McCall, Morgan W. Jr. High Flyers: Developing the Next Generation of Leaders. Harvard Business School Press, 1998.

(8) McCall, Morgan W. and George P. Hollenbeck. Developing Global Executives. Harvard Business School Press, 2002.

(9) Charan, Ram, Stephen Drotter and James Noel. The Leadership Pipeline: How to Build the Leadership-Powered Company. Jossey-Bass, 2001.

(10) Bunker, Kerry, Douglas T. Hall and Kathy E. Kram (Editors). Extraordinary Leadership: Addressing the Gaps in Senior Executive Development. John Wiley & Sons, 2010.

(11) Senge, Peter. The Fifth Discipline: The Art & Practice of the Learning Organization.Doubleday, 1990.

(12) Wheatly, Margaret. Leadership and the New Science. Berrett-Koehler, 2006.

(13) Pascale, Richard, Mark Millemann and Linda Gioja. Surfing the Edge of Chaos. Three Rivers Press, 2000.

(14) Olson, Edwin and Glenda Eoyang. Facilitating Organization Change: Lessons from Complexity Science. Jossey-Bass, 2001.

(15) Stacey, Ralph. Complexity and Creativity in Organizations. Berrett-Koehler, 1996.

(16) Heifitz, Ron. Leadership Without Easy Answers. Harvard University Press, 1994.

(17) Heifitz, Ron, and Marty Linksy. Leadership on the Line: Staying Alive through the Dangers of Leading. Harvard Business School Press, 2002.

(18) Mouawad, Jad. "Sticking the Landing." Minneapolis StarTribune, May 20, 2011, page D, 6.

(19) For an overview of scenario planning see <u>Scenarios: The Art of Strategic Conversations</u>. van der Heijden, Kees. Wiley, 2005, or <u>The Living Company</u>. De Geus, Arie, Harvard Business School Publishers, 2002 and Schrage, Michael, <u>Serious Play</u>, Harvard Business School Press, 2000. To find out more about storyboarding, which is a visual technique borne in the film industry to lay out future plot lines, go to your favorite search engine on the web and type in *storyboarding*. Also see *Painting Pictures of the Future,* in Kotter, John. <u>The Heart of Change</u>. Harvard Business School Press, 2002, pp. 62-67. Deep Dive is a technology used at IDEO Company, the world's leader in innovation and design. See Stone, Brad. "Reinventing Everyday Life." *Newsweek*, October 27, 2003 or go to IDEO.com.

Leading & Uncertainty

They (musical predecessors) were my teachers. They were great teachers because they didn't know they were teaching, they were just doing the next right thing. They taught with love and by example, without prejudice or guile, simply by being themselves.

Eric Clapton

My bookshelves are overflowing with books and articles on leadership. Most present leadership as a set of skills to be mastered. I get a sense as I read them that many of the authors believe that leaders also have some great and innate ability to be in a state of personal control in the most challenging of circumstances. Some leadership documentaries play off of the same lore. I watched the public television version of Sir Ernest Shackleton's epic journey again last night, for example. Time and again his descendants, the decedents of his shipmates and his personal notes on the voyage recalled that he was always calm and in control even during the most hazardous of leadership situations in his attempt to cross the South Pole early last century. The same is true of most first run movies whether it is Tom Hanks in *Apollo 13*, Mel Gibson in *Braveheart* or Pierce Brosnan as *007*. The new James Bond, Daniel Craig, in *Casino Royale* (based on Ian Fleming's first novel) and *Quantum of the Solace* show a different Bond, one more uni-dimensional and more of a mercenary rather than a leader.

My experience as a leader is different than the lore depicted above. Also, my consulting with leaders paints a different and less rosy picture of leadership during trying and uncertain times. While leaders often present their calm and in control "game face" to their organizations, their frustration, anger and feelings of insecurity are clear if you look more closely. Off line, they talk to trusted spouses, colleagues, friends or consultants about their sleepless nights, anxiety, feelings of inadequacy, fears and hopes. They seem more like the characters in the movies *Finding Nemo, Harry Potter, The Lord of the Rings and The King's Speech*. They each have a worthy goal, start a journey with others not sure exactly of what will happen next, step off into the unknown, and experience fully the emotional ups and downs of riding the waves of change and the uncertainty a significant challenge brings. Over time, they learn to understand and manage the emotions change brings and see change and uncertainty as a natural process to grow and learn from.

I recently asked three clients to comment on their thoughts and feelings about leading in uncertain times. I wanted to test my hypothesis that leaders often go to hell, as my friend and colleague ML says, during their leadership journeys. And, that they learn important life lessons from the suffering they experience along the way making them better leaders and persons as a result. Warren Bennis calls these trials leadership crucibles. I chose three very different people from three very different industries. The first is the president of a national restaurant chain, the largest in its segment. His business is in the process of being sold and he will probably lose his job. The second

52

is the president of a family held company that was purchased by a large, diversified, European, manufacturing company. He was given financial targets to meet but not told much about other expectations for his business. The third is an entrepreneur, President and CEO who formed a health care cooperative in Minnesota several years ago. His owners/members are seeking to refocus and streamline his organization given changes in health care. I posed the following question to them:

What challenges do you personally face and need to respond to as the leader of your organization as it is in the process of dramatic change?

Here is a summary of what I heard.

(1) Leadership in limbo is probably a good phrase to describe what happens between the day you announce a sale and the day you close the deal. As a CEO, you spend most of your time trying to present a picture of life after the acquisition, which has not been entirely defined. You try to put aside your own uncertainties in order to preserve the ongoing business and act as much as possible in a business as usual mode.

Having been involved in several merger/acquisition transactions through the years I've learned a few things. First among them is that honesty is the best policy. [But] never put anything in writing until you are absolutely sure that you'll be able to deliver same. Try to maintain as much of a business as usual mode as possible while looking into yourself and understanding that the uncertainties and emotions that you are feeling are present throughout the organization. That will help you understand and be more sensitive to what others are feeling. Finally, maintain a positive attitude.

(2) *We were uncertain as to what we could and could not do, what control we had over our own future, and what degree of freedom we had to set and carry out a strategic plan. Members of my management team and I wanted us to do more and be a better performer. We decided that we needed to face the uncertainties head-on and try to gain some control over our own destiny. We listed what we thought was in our control, what wasn't and what we were unsure of. We used these lists to guide our planning, helping to make it more realistic and meaningful. We decided that we needed to clarify our vision and purpose. But, we were also concerned that if we changed too abruptly, and too drastically, we could destroy the fabric of our culture. We communicated with our employees and involved many of them in our strategic planning process. We also reinforced our traditional values in this process.*

Once we defined our direction we then needed to restructure the organization and build some new competencies. We were not only successful ourselves, but we also helped the parent company define how it should structure itself worldwide. Now the parent company uses our model as the template for its other geographic business units. Looking back, I think I should have pursued more information from the company that purchased us, earlier on, about what their intent was in purchasing us. Leadership in times of uncertainty asks us all to head into it knowing that some mistakes will be made, but understanding that learning and growth will come from it. Staying with the status quo is never the right option. It sure wasn't for us.

(3) *This has been very trying for me personally. My board (the coop owners) seems, at times, to have lost sight of the fact that a coop works best when all of the members are utilizing the services that we provide. The reason we formed the coop was to leverage our buying power for the goods and services we all need. Now some of the members want to color outside of the lines and reach their own agreements with service providers outside of the coop structure. This harms the other members. While I see this happening, I also know that this is THEIR organization. It was created by many of them with my help and it should serve THEIR purposes. I need to keep reminding myself of that. Sometimes that is really hard for me. I find myself getting angry and frustrated. I don't show it that much. At least I don't think I do. I have decided that I need to take the role of the information provider, process facilitator and the person who will execute their will. I want to help them make decisions based in fact. As long as they do that, I will be happy with whatever they want to do.*

My staff knows what is going on as well. They have jobs that could be eliminated or altered significantly. And while they deal with the uncertainty of change, they/we need to continue to work with a high level of productivity and professionalism. I don't hide anything from them. They are adults and need information to plan their futures. At times I wonder if I want to be a part of the organization my board might be in the process of creating. If that becomes the case, I will not become a barrier to the changes they want to make. I will create another opportunity for myself. There is so much work that needs to be done in this industry.

Lessons Learned:

1. Leaders face difficult intellectual challenges during periods of change.
2. Leaders also experience deep emotions during the challenges they face.
3. Dealing with uncertainty is a reflective process that can take you to a personal hell creating a crucible of insight and learning about one's self and uncertainty.
4. This reflective growth process is at the heart of leadership development.
5. Leaders need to have confidants to talk with about the uncertainties they face.
6. Listen to, watch carefully and learn from leaders who are in the act of working through uncertainty and experimenting with growth, change and development.

4. *Perspective, Leadership and Culture*

Culture is the human response to physical, biological and other environmental conditions, prior history, assumptions, values and attitudes, psychological traits, social structure and present demands. If the responses are successful, the capacity to exist is maintained and maybe even increased. The response can be seen through individual behavior and the patterns, which form, over time, within human groups or across or between human groups.

Anthropologists have been studying this phenomenon for more than one hundred years. Those who have studied social and cultural changes have focused their work in two basic arenas. One type of study focuses on how a specific group of people has operated at a particular time in history. These works have attempted to gain an understanding of how culture is a patterned response to a complex set of dynamic factors over time. A classic example of this type of work (often called ethno-history or salvage anthropology) is E. Adamson Hoebel's The Cheyennes (1). Hoebel depicted the Northern Cheyennes of North America between 1840-60, prior to the western expansion by Europeans, when their nomadic life (and accompanying struggles) was slowing. Tribal elders were interviewed and asked to describe their culture as it had been when they were young children. They

> *"Change is not only inexorable, it is necessary."*
>
> Kwai Chaing Cane
> quoting Frank Zappa

were also asked to convey stories and events of the period that they had been told by others, including elders, at the time. Their ceremonies, social structure, hunting and gathering activities, worldview and personality were described in great detail to bring this time and group of people to life for us.

A second type of anthropological study are case studies of change, which focus on how groups and individuals have adapted to changes imposed by outside forces, usually human and technological in nature. These foundational change cases are often called forced change, as the individuals and groups were not given choice or much prior information regarding the changes that were coming. Pertti Pelto's study of how the Skolt Lapps of northeastern Finland adapted to the introduction of the snowmobile into their culture is one example of such a study (2). Utilizing snowmobiles instead of foot travel to herd caribou initiated a number of changes including the giving up of traditional ways for more modern social, economic, political and cultural practices. Another example is Robert Kiste's case of the forced movement of men, women and children from Bikini atoll in the Pacific by the American military, as the US needed the atoll for the testing of nuclear warheads (3). The people were a sea and fishing based culture who were moved to an environment where existence was based primarily on forestry and farming. The story tracks their forced movement, resettlement and return after the unsuccessful resettlement. A third example is Gregory Reck's study of personal choice and change in a small Mexican village where its isolation from outside forces such as electricity, a road and modern civilization was swiftly coming to an end (4). At the heart of these case studies is an attention to how humans solve problems or dilemmas in order to survive, physically, emotionally, spiritually and culturally. This idea of solving problems as a core element of culture is a major theme in many anthropological studies.

More recently, these anthropological concepts have found their way into the business management literature. The concept of culture came to business in 1982 via a book called Corporate Cultures: The Rites and Rituals of Corporate Life by Terry Deal and Allan Kennedy (5). This book and subsequent books by these authors gave insight into the concept of culture and its relevance for business people. They provided an overview of some of the key concepts, terms and how many organizational dilemmas could be better understood through the lens of culture. The New Corporate Cultures (6) provides insight into the effects of drastic organizational changes like downsizing, outsourcing, reengineering and mergers on organizational culture. Reframing Organizations (7), first published in 1991, is a textbook written for MBA students which discusses organizational culture, power, structure and human resources. It shows how widely available information on organizational culture has become for business people and happened so quickly.

In 1985, Edgar Schein wrote a book entitled Organizational Culture and Leadership (8). In the book he describes the role of founder-leaders in creating culture and subsequent leadership's needed role in discovering and altering the culture's basic premises in order for it to adapt and change in line with new social, political, technological or economic forces. A key point of his work notes that often what inhibits organizational changes are the implicit dimensions of culture (assumptions) that are no longer transparent to those who lead the firm. In a subsequent book Schein applied his ideas to DEC (Digital Equipment Corporation) where he describes the innovator's rise and fall. He chronicles the strength of their early culture becoming a burden later as they failed to anticipate the advent of the personal computer. This, and other problems, he says, led to their economic demise (9).He has also published a practical book on trouble shooting organizational culture issues in his Corporate Culture Survival Guide (10). More recently, the Dutch author, Fons Trompenaars, in his Riding the Waves of Cultural Change (11), helps us better understand multi-cultural dilemmas in international business transactions by showing us cultural differences along three broad dimensions; relationships, the passage of time, and our relationship to the environment. He asserts that mastering these dimensions improves leadership. Both Schein and Trompenaars state that a business culture is comprised of three levels or layers. The most visible layer includes the *artifacts* or products of the culture such as, in the US, packaged, ready to eat food, suburbs, shopping malls and the human behavior associated with them. These are the more explicit cultural factors. They are generally what most people see as culture. However, these artifacts are merely expressions of deeper *values and norms* in society that are not directly visible, such as convenience, status, material success and geographic mobility. These aspects of culture are deeper and more difficult to

"Humans are animals suspended in webs of significance they themselves have spun. I take culture to be those webs and the study of it to be therefore not an experimental science in search of law but an interpretive one in search of meaning (12)."

Clifford Geertz

"Culture is a system of things, social relations and ideas, a complex mechanism by which people exist and persist. It is organized not merely to order relations but to sustain human existence (13)."

Marshall Sahlins

discern, especially by current members of the culture. Over time, values and norms become invisible and non-conscious to those who live by them as they become accustomed to using them to solve dilemmas and problems presented to them. A conscious problem, regularly solved, falls from our conscious thought process, and over time becomes an unexamined *assumption*; a basic, *implicit* cultural premise. Purchasing convenience-oriented food products, for example, solves the problem of busy schedules and dual career families on the move. An interrelated collection or system of these basic premises forms the foundation of a culture's beliefs and fosters cultural processes, events and rituals. These activities create and reinforce the meaning and significance of life for those who share and live by the premises. As life's dilemmas are resolved by cultural activities, life continues on. Over time, assumptions, behavioral norms and artifacts become more intertwined and self-reinforcing, producing what anthropologists call a strong culture. However as new challenges arise, like they do in today's turbulent business world, new artifacts, values and assumptions are needed for constructive change, adaptation and new problem-solving to occur. Without new ways, cultures and businesses decline. Without the leadership perspective to accomplish these tasks, cultures and business are adrift in a sea of change without a rudder or navigation.

Corporate Culture, Leadership and Performance

The study of culture, called fieldwork by anthropologists, can help business leaders better understand groups and their behavior within their firms, their firm as a whole and the dynamics of their industry. One can also learn to better understand the interconnections between all of these aspects of work and life. We can also see to the core of certain issues we encounter such as why and how change initiatives succeed and fail. Many change efforts fail, for example, because change leaders stay at the explicit level of change, reengineering work systems and technology without first reengineering the implicit, basic, cultural premises which form the basis of culture. They focus on the relationship between corporate culture and business performance. As John Kotter states in his book <u>Corporate Culture and Performance</u> (14), there is a solid link between shareholder value and the intangible assets of a company. Firms often struggle to make the connection between culture (as a metaphor and measure of their operating model) and the direct impact it can have on shareholder value. Roger Connors and Tom Smith further this idea by focusing on the current issue of accountability and culture in their book <u>Change the Culture, Change the Game</u> (15). Culture creation and culture change skills are critically important for managers at all levels. Thus, leadership development, in part, is anthropological development.

For almost 100 years the anthropological record stayed in the academy. However, beginning in the 1980's, Deal and Kennedy brought many of the basic concepts or culture to the business community. Since then, a number of authors have applied their concepts and further analytical insights to organizational leaders. A key point is that leaders are often the least able to understand their own corporate culture. What they develop is often not done with a conscious mindset. And, even if consciously developed, the basic premises of an organizational culture drop into the implicit aspects of organizational life. They become simply the way we do things around here and are invisible. Their origins are lost, and often the cultural assumptions, beliefs and values drive behavior that at one point created success for the company only later become the reason for decline. A leadership perspective is based on an ability to consciously see, understand, interpret and adapt or change a corporation's culture to support business innovation and competitiveness.

Here are some key questions I have been asked by business leaders that can only be explained by concepts and techniques from the field of anthropology.

- What is wrong with the culture of our financial employees? They don't seem to be adding any value to the business.
- We are a new division of a conservative company growing our revenue stream by forty percent per year. How can we develop a culture that continues to emphasize creativity, risk taking, and innovation and not complacency?
- We have been having an extremely difficult time getting a business deal signed with our Chinese partner. Do you have any idea why this might be so?
- When I hold performance discussions with my Thai employees they don't seem to know what to say. Why is that?
- We are a new start up company. We have our senior

management team in place and are beginning to hire employees. How do we consciously develop a company culture that will serve our customers and be a great place to work?

- The culture we consciously developed as a start-up has eroded. Now we are an organization with an espoused culture that is far different from how we really operate. How can we work our way out of the abyss?
- Are business cultures of virtual firms different than those of more traditional ones?
- Our industry will change dramatically over the next five years. How can we improve our strategic thinking skills so we can meet the challenges we will face?
- How can we help our employees better understand business acumen?
- What do I need to do to keep myself fresh as a leader given the rapid pace of change and the uncertainty and stress that comes with it.

Now that you have a little bit better understanding of the rise of anthropological concepts and thought in business we will turn our attention to the mental processes that anthropologists acquire through their formal training and field assignments. Understanding and practicing these methods will improve culture alertness and insight. Mastering these processes will lead to a heightened state of mind and strategic thinking. Practice and development over time will develop and renew a robust leadership perspective.

Notes:

(1) Hoebel, E. Adamson. The Cheyennes: Indians of the Great Plains. Holt, Rinehart and Winston, 1960.

(2) Pelto, Pertti. The Snowmobile Revolution: Technology and Social Change in the Arctic. Cummings, 1973.

(3) Kiste, Robert. The Bikinians: A Study in Forced Migration. Cummings, 1974.

(4) Reck, Gregory. In the Shadow of Tlaloc: Life in a Mexican Village. Penguin, 1978.

(5) Deal, Terrance and Allan Kennedy. Corporate Cultures: The Rites and Rituals of Corporate Life. Perseus, 1982

(6) Deal, Terrance and Allan Kennedy. The New Corporate Cultures. Perseus, 1999.

(7) Bolman, Lee and Terrance Deal. Reframing Organizations: Artistry, Choice and Leadership (Fourth Edition). Jossey-Bass, 2008.

(8) Schein, Edgar. Organizational Culture and Leadership. Jossey-Bass, 1985.

(9) Schein, Edgar. Dec is Dead: Long Live Dec. Berrett-Koehler, 2003.

(10) Schein, Edgar. The Corporate Culture Survival Guide. John Wiley & Sons, 2009.

(11) Trompenaars, Fons. Riding the Waves of Cultural Change: Understanding Diversity in Global Business. McGraw-Hill, 1997.

(12) Geertz, Clifford. The Interpretation of Cultures. Basic Books, 1972, pg. 5.

(13) Sahlins, Marshall. "Remarks on Social Structure in Southeast Asia." *Journal of thePolynesian Society*, 1963, pg. 72.

(14) Kotter, John. Corporate Culture and Performance. The Free Press, 1992.

(15) Connors, Roger and Tom Smith. Change the Culture, Change the Game: The Breakthrough Strategy for Energizing Your Organization and Creating Accountability for Results. Portfolio, 2011.

Falling Leaves

To every season there is a purpose, under heaven.

Roger McGuinn
(from the *Book of Ecclesiastes*)

We experienced our first hard frost two weeks ago. A hard frost is defined as three or more hours when the temperature is at or below 28 degrees Fahrenheit. The next morning, as I worked at my computer, the large Ash tree in my front yard was dropping its leaves so quickly that it lost all of its leaves by 10 a.m. It happened so abruptly. There was no fall show of the leaves turning from green to bright yellow. It just went from green to bare in a few short hours.

I didn't notice it at first.

I was working frantically to cut and paste 40 strategy formulation surveys together and create a master survey for an international client's three day strategic planning session I was leading. I was absorbing their issues as I cut and pasted narrative ideas on industry dynamics and competitive issues. The billion-dollar company is in an industry fraught with over-capacity, declining margins, consolidation and certain product commoditization. In the last two years it had closed a dozen of its manufacturing plants and released one third of its employees. There was a new leadership team in place but their credibility was marginal given the wave of cost cutting, employee lay offs and the resulting low morale. They told me that they had completed their cost cutting and wanted to start a concerted effort to grow the company. "There is no one silver bullet," their president told me. The company would have to be efficient in their business fundamentals and look for opportunities to acquire businesses in more profitable niches than their current business.

Back to the leaves. They were really coming down fast now. I had to take a closer look. I stood at the base of the twelve inch diameter tree, standing in a shower of dying leaves. I felt a pang of sorrow. Fall is my favorite time of the year. I love the cold nights and the warm sunny days. I also am an amateur arborist and appreciate each of my trees that I chose and planted to provide a special affect be it their shape, size or fall color. I wondered why the Ash dropped its leaves so fast this and every year.

I realized that next spring the tree would push its new foliage out earlier that the others, as it does every year, and a new cycle of life would commence. But I was left with more questions. What did the tree's lineage and experience tell it about a competitive strategy for survival and continuity? What did this tree "know" about the winter to come? There were other Ashes in the neighborhood. They still had their leaves. Mine had chosen to lose its leaves early in preparation for what was to come... an early, hard winter? A conservative approach to the challenges posed by the shifts in seasons over its many years?

I returned back to my work. There were more surveys lighting up my email message system. The next few surveys described a tough business environment for more than a decade but only recent business closings and dislocated workers at the company. There were also some pokes at former management for their lack of attention to changes in technology and globalization that were reshaping the industry. Why hadn't the former leaders of the company realized that their forest was becoming populated with new hybrid trees and imports from around the world? Why did it take new individuals to realize that bigger changes, changes that should have taken place more naturally over several years, needed to be made to continue the cycle of life?

Businesses must deal with issues of death, growth and survival just as other organisms do in nature. However, we sometimes allow ourselves to feel like we are not subject to the laws of nature. We see ourselves as apart and above nature. We let arrogance grow during the good years and postpone difficult decisions during the marginal years. We live in this fantasy world until we have no choice but to induce changes that may put our companies at further risk. The mantra in the company above is that it will either grow or be purchased and chopped up by another competitor in the rush of industry consolidation.

Lessons learned:

1. Trim your business a little at a time as the industry seasons change so you don't have to over-prune and risk killing the organization during very difficult times.
2. Don't add staff and overhead as much as you would like during the especially fertile years.

3. Review your business cycles over the past few year as well as looking ahead a few years and see if you have a renewal and growth outlook.
4. Anticipate the changing nature of your industry and act before you have to.
5. Spend more time observing nature and extracting insights from the lessons it teaches us!

Epilogue. I reconnected with this company eight years later on another consulting assignment. Their business has improved as they have pushed their way up the value chain in their industry avoiding many of the low cost issues of a commodity business. Everyone I worked with eight years ago is gone. It is eerie to sit in an office of a high ranking employee, knowing that three people sat behind the same desk during the tumultuous years since I was here last. And, it feels odd to walk the halls and see all the empty cubes and offices showing the carnage of relentless cost cutting and layoffs. The culture is helter-skelter given so much turnover at all levels and so many new senior employees from so many different industries. However, what is most interesting is that the new employees have little or no knowledge of prior senior management team members, strategies and important initiatives. In fact, employees refer to the old days as *the dark days* and it is very difficult to get them to talk about those important years. Little do they know that the pain was unavoidable given their competitive situation at the time and their inability to distinguish the forest from the trees.

5. *Five Insights*

Anthropological thinking centers around five domains of thought and inquiry, referred to here as insights. After years of academic study and completing numerous fieldwork projects where they live and study in a culture different from their own, anthropologists develop and hone these mental routines. As you will see, these insights are actually intertwined. They are a mindset. After this rigorous training, these mental and behavioral methods or processes are no longer conscious, just as the thinking and behavior of biologists specializing in infectious diseases or attorneys specializing in contract law are no longer conscious to them. They become a part of the person.

The thought processes presented here may seem to you to be a little awkward or uncomfortable at first. With practice, however, the processes will become more natural feeling for you. After some time, many individuals say that the insights are a part of their thinking process. However, they have never had names for them before or thought in a deeper way about developing their perspective. Practice the exercises presented in the book. Over time, you can learn to see the world through the eyes of a cultural anthropologist. This will be especially handy when you need a different and better perspective. And, it will accelerate your leadership development and refresh your leadership perspective as needed.

5.1. _Look Beneath the Surface_

I have two children who both have played traveling basketball when they were young. (Traveling basketball is non-school sponsored basketball for fifth to eighth graders. When funding was cut to school-based athletic programs in the 1980's and 1990's, parents formed non-profit clubs to pick up the responsibility. Traveling basketball, in most school districts across the country, offers more games, more tournaments, more competition and stronger developmental opportunities for young athletes. Athletes participate through their school's athletic programs for high school athletics.) Each of my two children played a combined number of about seventy-five games (league and tournament) over four months. In addition, I was one of the coaches on my son's team, which meant that I attended an average of two practices per week in addition to the games. I was also on the club board and the director of the annual club tournament.

I spent a great deal of time with the traveling program. As I talked with basketball parents at and between practices and games I came to know many of the parents of the players quite well. Many of these parents spent as much time as I did with this sport. I am truly surprised, though, that few parents, given the amount of time they spent on basketball related activities, attempted to learn more about the game's rules, strategies or physical demands. Of course there are a few parents who wanted more information and wanted to go deeper. But most did not. The parents who did choose to become more involved offered to run the time clock or keep the official score book at games. Others watched practice and talked to the coaches to learn more. When I asked the parents who did get more involved why they did it they said that they wanted to know more as they were not involved in athletics when they were young. They wanted to learn more so they could participate in and appreciate the challenges and joys of their children.

A few years ago, my son and his high school team won the Minnesota State High School Championship. As I looked through the Target Center crowd after the game, I noticed how many parents had attended so many games over the years. The ones who had truly sought to understand the game, the amount of hard work and dedication that their son had put in and the enormous feat that they had accomplished, smiled a smile of insight and meaning. The others who had merely attended games but were not involved in the learning and appreciation process seemed excited but bewildered by the spectacle and the meaning of it all. They missed a huge opportunity to learn and grow as parents. And, their memories probably will not be as full and meaningful as those of the parents who were engaged fully in the process.

The World is a Learning Laboratory

Opportunities to learn present themselves to us in business as well as in life in general. But some of us do not seem to notice. Some of us wait to be asked to learn, while others are more curious, active learners who do not wait to be asked. A corporate executive friend of mine has become frustrated with employees who are not self-starting, active learners. He once said, "Our company is a learning lab waiting for employees to discover it. For example, there are teams and taskforces studying important issues which employees could volunteer to join but don't. And, there are job opportunities which we end up filling from outside of the company because we do not have internal candidates ready and skilled to do the job." He makes a good point. A teaching colleague who teaches leadership courses suggests that the first step in becoming a leader is to have leadership intent. We must choose to see the world as a learning lab. We must look beneath the surface of the situations we are in and, when important to us, go deeper to understand the basic premises that drive them.

Many of us get caught in learning ruts and pay attention to only a small part of the world around us, what for us is easiest and nearest to us given our experience, training and social location or position. All too often, in my opinion, speed and time are the key culprits in the prevention of the development of perspective. I'm reminded of the "speedboaters" and the "sailboaters" my friend John Cowan (1, 2) writes about. The "speedboaters" are concerned primarily with getting from point A to point B in the shortest possible amount of time. The "sailboaters," in contrast, are more concerned with experiencing the process of getting from point A to point B. Both have an appreciation of *time* and *the experience* as key variables in boating. However, the "sailboaters" can give you a more detailed understanding of wind and water conditions. They also can give you a more complex understanding of navigational strategy as more than full throttle. Can you really see and understand anything except the adrenaline rush of *time x experience* if you live and manage at full throttle? Taking an intentional, active approach to learning from the world around us is the first important step in gaining perspective. Looking beneath the surface to deeper realities is a first behavioral step in building your perspective.

Jeffrey Kluger, in his book Simplexity: Why Simple Things Become Complex (and How Complex Things Can Be Made Simple) (3), looks beneath the surface of a cholera epidemic, predicting the stock market, the patterns of people fleeing a burning building and other social, economic and political matters. He turns them upside down and inside out to show us how things really work. He believes that humans lack the ability to see the simplicity in complex situations like a cholera epidemic and to appreciate the complexity of a simple thing like a pencil. Being able to distinguish what is simple from what is complex refines and enriches one's perspective on the world we live in.

Thus, we are confused by beauty, by speed, by big numbers, by small numbers, by our own fear, by wealth, by eloquence, by size, by success, by death, by the unfathomability of life itself. There is a taxonomy of things that fools us every day and, in so doing, helps the complex masquerade as the simple, and the simple parade itself as complex (3, page 16).

Anthropologists are given assignments in their early coursework to stop and notice what goes on around them. One of my professors, for example, gave me the assignment of studying fire hydrants in the Dinkytown area near the University of Minnesota. I, like thousands of students before and after me, walked by those artifacts of urban America several times per day. And, I, for one, had never really noticed them before. I became an expert in the shapes, sizes and distances from each other, storefronts and other physical entities in the next ten weeks. By taking a more analytical posture, I soon realized that fire hydrants had their own history of technological development and innovation illustrated by their size and design. Understanding their history gave me some insight into the historical development of Dinkytown. And, their placement, which seemed random at first, also gave me a retrospective view of the early layout of the streets and buildings. It is easier to remake a storefront or reroute a street or alley than to alter the city's fire abatement design! The key learning point was not about fire hydrants or urban geography. It was about what we pay attention to and why. It was also about the consequences of not appreciating what is around us.

In the graduate business classes I teach I ask business students to do similar studies. I was lucky enough a few years ago to teach a course for a university MBA program in a classroom at The Mall of America, which is one of the world's largest indoor shopping and entertainment centers. Rather than separate the class from the Mall, I chose to integrate them so that students would be encouraged to stop, notice and look into things that they normally would pass right by. The purpose of the assignments was to gently nudge students to look beneath the surface and develop a keener sense of observation. For example, in one of the first sessions, after introducing the concepts of active learning, I asked if anyone had done a study of doorways. After the laughter subsided, I asked the students to do the following assignment in teams of five.

Doorway Culture Study

Find a central, glass doorway with heavy foot traffic which you can see through in a business or retail store. It is best to use a downtown or mall location. Choose a place where you can observe the people entering and leaving the building through the glass doors. You should be close enough so that you can see the expressions on their faces. Watch as people approach the doorway. Start by watching people enter. Then watch as people leave. Do this for fifteen minutes noting any patterns you see. Now pay special attention to two types of encounters. First, look for two or more people entering through the doorway together. Who opens the door for whom? Second, watch for situations where individuals approach the doorway from different sides (outside and inside). What protocol is used to determine who passes through the doorway first? Do this for fifteen minutes more. Reflect on what you have just observed. What have you learned about the culture of doorways? Does it mean anything in a larger sense about social relations in your community or society in general?

The business students were truly amazed at how many things they observed when they actually took the time to stop and patiently observe.

- There was no eye contact between strangers.
- Adults allowed children to go first through the doorways.
- Groups approaching from each side of the exterior door would choose an alternative door thus avoiding any potential conflict based on who was the nearest to or furthest from the entry. Those individuals who were furthest would defer to those individuals or groups closer to the door.
- Many (but not all) women proceeded through the doors first except when children were present or when it was a group of mixed (male and female) adolescents.
- Some individuals truly were on a mission with speed, intent, experience and skill. They deftly darted and squirted through the crowds and doorways almost in hyper-speed.

Culture in a public place such as a mall is about the meaning of things in the particular setting among the people who interact there. When I asked the students about their observations and what they meant, they talked about the impersonal nature of human interactions in public places between strangers. "We live in a time when you stick to your group for safety reasons," many elaborated. "A large public space is not like a neighborhood snack shop where we all know each other," one student said. "You have to be careful." The students also talked about the roles of children and women in American society. They observed that children have a special place in the hearts of adults and go through the doors first in a kind of importance sequence. In addition, they saw that the role of women is changing as illustrated by the fact that they did not always follow the children through the doorway. Sometimes they led. The "hyper-speed people" were icons of today's fast-paced lifestyle multitasking their way through the doorways in the most time efficient (and impersonal) manner.

Why could we gain so much perspective on American life by merely observing doorway behavior for thirty minutes? Because doorways are microcosms of life. So, through this simple exercise we observe some emerging elements of the suburban scene in America after careful observation of some human activities in doorways. Something on the periphery of our interest is complex, yet simple if one takes the time to try to understand it.

I have taught this exercise at a downtown campus location and in a small town setting as well. Students who cannot attend the class because of business travel complete the exercise wherever they are. I have learned that doorway cultures differ depending on where they are located, the architecture of the building, the function of the space (office, retail, multipurpose, etc.) and the culture of the participants. Students report a heightened awareness of doorways and other social situations as a result of this exercise. Many also state that when they are in an important situation at work such as a goal setting meeting, a company party or their performance review that they can actually turn on their observational antenna to gain some additional perspective. This helps them ask an insightful question or make an important observation.

Outliers

Malcolm Gladwell, in his book <u>Outliers</u> (4) provides compelling research about how successful people distinguish themselves from others. He looks beneath the argument that successful people are so because of intelligence and ambition. The lives of outliers—those people whose achievements fall outside normal experiences—he argues, are determined by opportunity, generation, family, culture and class. He also talks about *The 10,000 – Hour Rule*. Gladwell doesn't dispute the notion of innate talent. To talent he adds preparation. Thus, success is talent plus preparation.

The idea that excellence at performing a complex task requires a critical minimum level of practice surfaces again and again in studies of expertise. In fact, researchers have settled on what they believe is the magic number for true expertise: ten thousand hours (4, pages 39-40).

He provides examples such as how many hours The Beatles logged in clubs in England and Germany before coming to America and Bill Gates' doing real-time programming as an eighth grader in 1968, just as the computer era was getting started. Remember the concept of the gym rat? You know, the kid who shoots baskets before practice and after practice then goes to the park dribbling her basketball along the way only to return home and compete against her older male siblings in a grudge match in the driveway? Yes. The Beatles, Bill Gates and many of the kids who won their state basketball tournament were rats of one type or another:

club, computer room or gym. To be successful, one must have talent and obsession with achievement, but also must do the work.

Successful leaders, in my experience, have talents that are important to leadership success such as intelligence, interpersonal skills, adaptability, a strong goal orientation, etc. Very few, however, succeed the first time they find themselves in the leadership situation and every time after that. They have an almost obsessive intention to lead, they seek out leadership situations to practice, learn and grow and they started at an early age so they have put in their Gladwell hours. The need to be leadership rats and their place of endeavor is the workplace.

Developing leadership perspective requires the same logic as becoming successful in other arenas. Looking beneath the surface necessitates practice. So, choose situations that you encounter frequently but don't pay much attention to like fire hydrants or doorways. Observe these location or places as you encounter them with the conscious intention of learning more about them. Have two or three studies going on simultaneously. Give the study a month or two of attention until you see patterns and gain insights you didn't have before. Then start new studies. Make this a part of your daily or weekly routine.

Here is a list of possible topics to get you thinking about a study to begin to get you beneath the surface.

- The Health Club. When exercising at your gym, pay

attention to how many people are there at a given time and how they are distributed among various areas. What are their demographics such as age, gender, ethnicity and income. Are some regulars or infrequent visitors? Do people come together or alone? What exercises do they do and how long do they spend at the gym? Who interacts with whom?

- The Grocery Store. When buying groceries at a supermarket where there are individuals who take your groceries to the car for you, strike up a conversation with them. Start by asking them how they are or how the day is going for them? Let them do the talking. Try to get a different bag person from time to time to get to know a variety of individual workers. As you develop a bit of a relationship with them, ask them what it is like to have their job and why they have chosen that type of work to do.

- The Staff Meeting. Start paying attention to more than the agenda and conversation at a staff or project meeting you attend frequently. Who arrives first, second and so on? Do employees arrive singly or in groups? Who sits where? Do individuals sit in the same spot each time? Who talks most frequently to least frequently? What topics engage the energy of each individual? Which do not?

To develop this skill it is quite important to understand the significance of looking beneath the surface and to practice active learning. Choose situations in your personal, social and business life in which you are currently on the surface, something you experience frequently but only pay cursory attention to. Look more closely. Observe patiently for fifteen to thirty minutes at a time. First, describe the physical setting. Then describe the activity you see (observations) in detail. Next, review your detailed observations noting any patterns. Finally, note the significance of the patterns. The patterns may not be easily seen in your first or second encounter. Be patient.

At the end of this section, use <u>Table 5.1.1 Observation Table</u> as a template to help you organize your observations and thoughts into a structured observation format. *Basic Description* asks you to write down what you see and hear. For example, if you are studying the culture of a coffee shop, you might draw a sketch of the layout of the local area around it and of the layout of the inside of the coffee shop itself. Then you could describe the furniture and other elements of the décor and the people. As you describe these things write down your commentary about what you see and hear (the descriptions) in the section titled *Observations*. The *Patterns* section asks you to step back and note the relationships you can discern across the descriptions and observations. Perhaps you notice that the coffee shop is divided informally into areas comprised separately of families with small children taking a break from their schedule for a snack and adults having a business meeting with their laptops open while looking at written documents. You also observe that the coffee order and pick up areas are within the family area that is quite noisy. The patterns are starting to emerge as you notice that the family section is full and there are only two tables that are occupied in the "business section." A family of three has just entered the

84

coffee shop, ordered and picked up their order of coffee and snacks. The mom looks around and seems confused as to where to sit. She guides her children to a table outside the door. The pattern might be that this is a coffee shop frequented primarily by small families during this time of day. It also appears that there is an area where business people sit during this time of day as well. Even though there is space for families to sit in the "business section" one family steers clear of the area and proceeds outside which acts as an overflow space. Now move on to the *Significance* area. What is significant about the descriptions, observations, and patterns you just discovered?

A Note on Significance

Significance is derived in different ways for the active researcher of social and business life (5). The first type of significance is what is important to those who are participants in the social setting or culture. Why do they think and act as they do? Does the person who rushes through the doorway do so because he is hurried? If there are sub groups, significance can be different for each sub group. A second type of significance can be found in how the different sub groups view themselves in relation to the other groups or how they view the other sub groups in relation to themselves. How do the fast-paced doorway people view slower moving groups? How do slower moving groups view others? Both of these types of significance are from the cultural participant's point of view.

A third type of significance is from the observer's point of view. What does the observer see and what does it seem to mean? The observer needs to be acutely careful of bias while assessing significance. Students, for example, often judge the slower moving doorway people as "lacking a purpose." They, as fast paced walkers, see the world in a similar way to those they observe. The key is to observe without judgment. Slower walkers certainly have a purpose. It might just be a little different that the faster paced walkers. The fourth type of significance is comparative. After studying doorway cultures at different retail stores, malls, etc., the observer can now make statements about the similarities and differences between them. Only then can the observer talk about doorway cultures in general or big malls versus small malls, rural versus urban, etc. One needs the data collected during the research to be able to make comparisons. The fifth level of significance is theoretical significance. The research is documented and compared to other scholarly work. Meaning, significance and future research ideas are developed. Types three, four and five are primarily from the observer's point of view supplemented with academic literature. These higher levels of significance must be grounded in types one and two – from inside the culture.

A trap many beginners fall into is deriving the outsider's point of view before they understand the point of view of an insider. It is mandatory to build the levels of significance from one through five in that order. It important to begin your work on the left side of the chart and work to the right. You must ground your observations in your actual descriptions rather than assuming you know what is going on in a socio-cultural setting. Patterns can only ascertained after describing and observing. Significance can only be determined after describing, observing, and noting patterns.

Sometimes your observations will lead to further research. What are the names of those employees in the coffee line? What part of the company do they work in? Do they come through the line every day at the same time? Do they always sit at the same table in the cafeteria? To hone this skill of looking beneath the surface, choose something once per week to observe or learn more about. If you do, you will gain deeper insights and broaden your perspective. And, if your kids play a musical instrument or a sport, learn by doing! Take a musical lesson or ask to get more involved in the sport.

Table 5.1.1. Observation Table

Basic Description	Observations	Patterns	Significance

Notes:

(1) Cowan, John. Small Decencies. HarperBusiness, 1992.
(2) Cowan, John. The Common Table. HarperBusiness, 1993.
(3) Kluger, Jeffrey. Simplexity: Why Simple Things Become Complex (and How Complex Things Can Be Made Simple). Hyperion, 2008.
(4) Gladwell, Malcolm. Outliers: The Story of Success. Little, Brown and Company, 2008.
(5) Significance as describe here is very different from statistical significance used in the quantitative sciences. For more information see Kirk, Jerome and Marc Miller. Reliability and Validity in Qualitative Research. Sage Publications, 1986 or Bernard, Russell and Gery Ryan. Analyzing Qualitative Data: Systematic Approaches. Sage Publications, 2010, or go to http://www.computing.dcu.ie/~hruskin/RM2.htm.

Run as the City Awakens

We run because we must.

Pierre Elliot Trudeau

"But the traffic, the heat, the crowds the uneven pavement," I think to myself. "Not to worry, John, we'll run as the city awakens. See you at 5:45. G'nite," said Gordon, "And don't be late." Gordon, my colleague from Melbourne, Australia, and I would run the next morning at 5:45 a.m. through the streets of Chiang Mai, Thailand which is 800 miles north of Bangkok. We planned to run through the city to the edge of town and into the foothills of the mountains bordering Thailand and Myanmar (formerly called Burma). This would happen during the week-long celebration of the 700th birthday of the city.

I am not a marathoner. My legs are sore when I awaken, but I'm past my jet lag and I can't say no. There is nothing like exploring 700 years of history in an hour or so on foot with a good friend and colleague.

A cool, light drizzle falls washing the air leftover from yesterday as we emerge from our hotel. The aroma of automobiles, buses, tuk tuks, food stalls and the Chiang Mai sewer system that has been mixed with the noise and hubbub of 21st century life in northern Thailand is washed so another day can begin. We follow the hotel access road to the main road and proceed north. Immediately we must cross the road as the sidewalk is blocked by a construction fence. It is dark and very quiet. The few street lights available to help us navigate our way are dim by American standards. They cast a shadow of light through the hazy mist, whereas their American counterparts illuminate sizable areas of darkness. A few bicyclists speed by to an unknown destination. A tuk tuk rushes to search for the first passengers of today or the last holdover of yesterday's evening. "Watch out," Gordon says. I leap to avoid a bicyclist carrying another bicycle across and perpendicular to his handlebars. I'd never seen anyone do that before. "Thanks, I didn't see him coming," I say. We shift from the street to the decaying sidewalk. Then we shift quickly back to the street to find more suitable footing and to avoid the telephone poles, gas meters and phone booths which seem to be forced irregularly in sidewalk placements detrimental to the safety of average Thai pedestrians but more so for two guys running in the dark.

The streets and sidewalks of Chiang Mai reveal all of their 700 years of archaeology to the feet, joints and legs of a 40 something year-old runner. Safety is first, especially when you are 10,000 miles from home and all you have to prove your identity is a room key from the Lotus Hotel. Looking up I spot one of the infrequent streetlights which illuminates the walls of the old city. The ancient walls are crumbling red brick and mud. My attention shifts to the context of my run, Chiang Mai, in Asia's Fertile Crescent. I try to imagine what life was like here 700 years ago.

The history of this place comes back to me. Buddhism, opium, the Vietnam war, the killing fields, the beauty. Our direction changes again as we dodge two brand new 5 Series BMW's loading up with affluent young Thais dressed in the latest European and Asian fashions. They seem to be beginning their return home from a night's partying. The sudden and dramatic contrasts of Thailand abound around me; the riches and the poverty, the old and the new, the beauty and the ugliness coexisting together as one Thailand.

The mist subsides.

"I must concentrate on the run," I remind myself. I am having difficulty keeping up with Gordon who is a younger and better-conditioned athlete. "I must forge ahead as we are nearing the road that will take us past the zoo and into the foothills which lead to Myanmar." The first sign of light is apparent and somehow I get a surge of energy. The sweat rolls down my back. We pass a sidewalk food vendor lighting her charcoal fire preparing unknown delicacies for those pedestrians who will soon be waking and entering the city to work. She has pots, bowls, two woks and a crate of the food she will prepare. I feel a bit hungry.

Now we get some elevation. It is slight at first, hardly noticeable, but enough to challenge me to focus and work harder to keep up with Gordon who is running smoothly a few paces ahead of me. I notice it isn't quite as dark as it was just a moment ago.

Coming into sight a quarter of a mile ahead of us we see a long procession of Buddhist Monks in their saffron robes. They are all carrying clay pots the size of a bushel basket. Each pot is equipped with a lid. Some Monks carry their pots in front of themselves with both hands using their stomachs as a third hand. Others have

the pot perched on a shoulder using their hand for balance. As Gordon and I approach, their leader, barefoot and bald, like all of his mentees, smiles as we pass. "The ancient one," I mutter to myself, recalling an American T.V. show called *Kung Fu: The Legend Begins*. The rest of the Monks do not make eye contact with us. We are going to the mountains and they toward the city. As we continue to pass the procession that seems like it is half a mile long or longer, my curiosity awakens as to where they are going and what the clay pots are for. There are many boys and some old men. Others are in their teens, twenties, thirties and more.

Gordon jolts me out of my inner world by announcing that he can hear the sound of rushing water and see a small bridge ahead. As I look past the bridge I see smoke from morning fires rising above a small village of thatched roofed dwellings. A dog barks, signaling that morning is approaching the village. A moment later we hear a rooster crow. Gordon and I smile to each other. We both know we are on the run of our lives.

As we enter the small village we see the monastery and the last of the Monks. They are lighting candles and placing them on an outdoor altar. They then turn and join the long line of robes ahead of them. Men, women and children begin to come out of their homes. A woman grabs a broom made of branches and begins to sweep her front stoop. Her husband stretches and looks to the sky as if to ascertain the day's weather forecast. "Time to turn back," Gordon states. Exhausted yet exhilarated, I nod my agreement.

Return runs always seem to go faster than out runs to me, whether I am in Minneapolis, Amsterdam, Sao Paulo or Chiang Mai. Is it that the uncertainty—the pavement, the weather, the air and the sights are not known at first? "Yes," I say to myself. "Maybe it is the process of anticipating what the unfamiliar will be like and then getting ready to experience it which is so difficult." The anticipation plus the actual experience of running in an unfamiliar land is what makes a run like this so anxiety producing yet so invigorating. The greater the unknown, the greater the anxiety, but also the greater the chance of having a positive, significant experience as well. The return run brings one back through the familiar to more and more known experiences, whether it is the hotel or home. This is the key to personal learning; encouraging oneself to push beyond what is comfortable, to look beneath the surface, to reflect upon it and to act on the insights derived from the experience. Some hope life's experiences will take them back to the familiar, rather than to a new place. What a pity.

Uphill running has become downhill running as we return toward the city retracing our steps. We cross the river and join the Monks again, but something is changing. There are people placing food into the Monk's pots: a potato, an onion, a vegetable I do not recognize. Individuals kneel at their feet, say a silent prayer, open the lid of the pot and place the food into the pot. The Monks are motionless and silent; eyes to the ground. People from the city have driven their automobiles out to this point to engage them. "Why do they do this," I wonder? The anthropologist in me stirs to suggest that the Monks must eat, but that in addition, they are spiritual beings to other Buddhists. They have taken a vow of poverty. They have committed their life to their journey. And, they are symbols of the way life should be lived for all Buddhists. Those offering gifts of food are truly feeding the Monks. And they are praying through the Monks to their god for peace, serenity and whatever personal guidance they need. Ahead I see the ancient one approach us. Both of us have gone full circle. He goes back to his village monastery and a day of prayer and solitude. I return to my hotel, a shower and a day of business meetings. As we pass, the ancient one and I acknowledge each other, seemingly recognizing in each other a kindred spirit that ties our lives together with some kind of cosmic purpose. We will meet tomorrow as we did this morning, but not the next, as I will return home.

I can hear the noise of Chiang Mai's traffic rise ahead. The sidewalks are filling with people on their way to work. The street vendor we passed is now selling food to hungry patrons. The heat is rising as is the noise, smog and life of the city. Our hotel is ahead. Gordon and I smile to each other, shake hands and slow down to walk up the steps toward the Lotus Hotel, exhilarated and ready to start our day.

Lessons Learned:

1. Push yourself out of your comfort zone.
2. Get out of the hotel.
3. Interact with the landscape.
4. Get into a learning mode by looking beneath the surface.
5. Enjoy!

5.2. *You are a Part of the Cultural System You are Participating In*

A few years ago, as you just read in *Run as the City Awakens*, I attended a meeting of Asia Pacific human resource professionals of a large global company in Chiang Mai, Thailand. During a break in the meeting, I introduced myself to an individual from Mainland China. He in turn introduced me to his colleagues who were all Chinese but either from Hong Kong or Taiwan. After a few minutes of small talk, I asked a question that I was very interested in. I asked how they felt about Hong Kong being returned to Mainland Chinese rule. Once I asked the question, I could tell by the looks on their faces that it made them uncomfortable. After a long pause, one gentleman replied, "We must work together but that does not mean we have chosen to talk about the politics of China." Then he turned around and talked to someone else without saying another word to me. I had obviously stepped on a cultural live wire without knowing it. This was an unfortunate event as the attendees from China, Hong Kong and Taiwan were cool toward me for the remainder of the conference. My friends back home in the states talk freely about political events and issues which is also the case in many places in Europe and Latin America. But not here. I relearned a lesson that seems trite but is very significant. Whether you are aware of it or not, just as the culture you are in influences you, you influence the cultural system you participate in.

We influence the cultural systems we participate in positively and negatively. We are neutral parties infrequently. However, many of us are unaware of the subtleties of this fact. Many of us are also more attentive to how others affect situational events around themselves than of our own effect. Being more conscious of these facts and exploring their ramifications is a second important part of growing and deepening your perspective. Most adults have learned and relearned this fact throughout their lives. But very few of us attempt to explore this point consciously and learn in more detail what this really means.

The problem is that many of us only learn about our influence when a problem arises as in my faux pas described above. Have you ever unknowingly committed a social indiscretion such as this? Did you stop and think about it to better understand what just happened? Or did you just go on with life? Hopefully you stopped to think. The Chinese event in particular has been a significant, personal learning event for me in a second way. During a recent MBA course I was teaching, I received an email note from a Chinese student who was reading an earlier version of this manuscript. (See next page). My indiscretion became clearer to me. Not only was this a touchy subject but she (and probably my Chinese colleagues) didn't want an American asking such a local, regional and personal question in a group setting. Learning from these experiences helps us see ourselves from other points of view be they from an individual's or a culture's point of view. Consciously seeing yourself as a part the system you are in or studying is an important factor in learning about activities in cross-cultural situations. I sent Martha a thank you card in the mail. Reflecting on situations such as this and extracting learning is an important step in gaining self-awareness in social settings. It is easier to see someone else's limitations or indiscretions, especially when we work with them every day. But it is more important to your interpersonal effectiveness to analyze yourself.

Dear Dr. Mirocha,

I am enjoying very much your book. I especially like the fact that you know that the center of the universe is not in your backyard as you illustrate in your *Lost Luggage* story. However, I would like to offer one thought to your understanding of the problem you had with the Chinese people when you were in Asia. Many Chinese are very tired of Americans thinking that they know everything about government, politics and society. They also become frustrated and angry that Americans seem to want to tell the world how to think and act when they have so many problems of their own and they have so little history to go by. I think you encountered this with your Chinese colleagues. I don't think that they wanted an American to lead a discussion of a Chinese political issue especially as you were in Asia. I hope this will help you with your perspective.

Respectfully, Martha

Theories-In-Use

Chris Argris and David Schon (1, 2) argue that individual behavior is controlled by personal theories for action – assumptions that inform and guide behavior. They describe two types of theories. *Espoused theories* are accounts individuals provide whenever they try to describe, explain or predict their behavior. *Theories-in-use* guide what people actually do. A theory-in-use is an implicit logic or set of rules and guidelines that specifies how to behave. Their research found significant differences between *espoused theories* and *theories-in-use*, which means that individuals' self-descriptions are often different or disconnected from their actions. Managers, for example, typically see themselves as more rational, open, concerned for others and democratic than they are seen by their employees. This blindness (blind spot) is persistent because people don't learn well from their experience. The biggest block to self awareness and the learning from experience that drives it is self-protection. Many individuals block feedback from the environment that breaks through the discrepancies between our espoused theories and our theories-in-use.

Just knowing this helps us understand that this discrepancy is natural and that we need feedback from others to be able to see the mismatches in our espoused theories and our theories-in-use. Seeking feedback to learn and grow is a part of recognizing that you are a part of the cultural systems you participate in. Seeing how others see us can provide constructive information to break down our self defenses. It can also provide for a good laugh, albeit at our own expense. Martha's honest feedback helped me see

"After all, had not he—Celistino de la Cruz— already gained countless valuable bits of information from the dictionary? He had learned that North America was connected to Mexico and that one did not have to travel by boat to get there as he once had thought. He was convinced that his knowledge of such things would eventually help him acquire what he desired—a store and a good reputation, so that people would respect him. He had received the dictionary from a medical student who was required to complete an internship in a community that lacked adequate health care. Before the intern left to establish a permanent practice elsewhere, he gave Celistino a box of medicine, a pharmaceutical encyclopedia, a pregnancy calendar, and the dictionary. Such was the legacy left by one of Celistino's true heroes, a man who was successful in the terms of a world that Celistino was struggling to make his own (3)."

Gregory Reck

that my international experience to that point was not relevant in Asia and that I needed to keep learning.

The Gods Must Be Crazy

Ideas, technology and artifacts shared across cultures can influence people and events as well. Anthropologists call this process cultural diffusion. Sometimes the consequences are positive for the culture and sometimes they can be negative. This point was the subject of the 1981 film entitled "The Gods Must Be Crazy," by Jamie Uys, which was the first version of a new Afrikaans-language film in Botswana. It proved so successful in South Africa that it was dubbed into English and re-released for the US market in 1984. It soon became the highest-grossing foreign film in American history. The film tells a story of an African Bushman whose serene and cooperative tribal life is torn apart. It all starts when a thoughtless bush pilot flying over the Kalahari Desert throws an empty Coke bottle out of his airplane window, landing quite literally on top of the Bushman's head.

The Bushmen are a nomadic group who believe that all physical possessions are owned communally. Many nomadic people have few possessions in the first place because having too many things makes it more difficult to move, set up and break camp, and transport things.   The Coke bottle is mistaken by the Bushman and his family and his tribe as a gift from the gods. The object becomes highly valued and is quickly put to use. In addition to being useful as a vessel for liquids it can also be used to magnify the Sun's rays to make fire and as an object to pulverize roots into powder. But it soon threatens to destroy the very fiber of the tribal group's harmonious culture. Family members become jealous of one another and compete, for the first time ever, to gain sole possession of the bottle. The discord goes on until Xi, the hero, decides that the gods had been severely misguided in giving him the Coke bottle. He then sets of on a trek to return the gift launching a series of misadventures that make up most of the bulk of the movie.

In addition to influencing culture directly through our actions and the introduction of a new artifact (intended or unintended), we can also influence events and relationships by not being in a certain place when it would be natural for us to be there. We are not trained to think of what does or does not happen as a result of changing our schedule or priorities, unless of course something significant happens.

The Man Who Missed the Flight

I met a man who, three years prior to our meeting, missed a flight because he was running late and got caught up in traffic in an unfamiliar city as he drove his rental car back to the airport. He started to tell me this as we waited in line to have our boarding passes scanned. I guess that is what got him started talking to me. He was a bit sweaty and a little out of breadth as he drove past the rental car return and got caught up in the traffic loop around the airport return road. He told me that he had a similar situation three years earlier in another airport and was glad he actually missed his flight that day. The flight he was originally schedule to fly on crashed on its landing. A number of the passengers did not survive the crash. If the flight he missed had landed safely he probably would not have given that flight another thought. Now he spends a great deal of time trying to understand why this happened to him and what, if anything, it means. He carries his original boarding pass with him as a reminder of what could have been. And he told me that he always wants to arrive at the airport he is embarking from early and that he worries a lot when he has to rush to make his flight. He wonders if chance will be his friend or foe if there is a next time.

As you can see from these examples, it is important to understand better the significance of our actions on other individuals and groups. As a special note, it is easier to gauge the significance of our effect on others in a cross-cultural setting than in one close to home because the cultural differences are usually so pronounced. However, while it is more difficult to determine our effect on those close and familiar to us, it is more important since this is where we spend the majority of our time and energy.

In addition to becoming more aware of our effects on others, we must learn to anticipate and manage our actions for the effect we desire. Anthropologists have studied their effects on others in cross-cultural settings for many years. They are trained to minimize their visibility and impact when they are involved in cross-cultural research activities. Yet, they realize that their mere presence can have an unintended effect on an individual or group. They are careful to observe and understand without altering the course of events as they would play out if they were not there in the first place, like the prime directive in the television series and movies of *Star Trek* and *Star Trek: The Next Generation (4)*.

While this strategy works for anthropologists, it may not be the best strategy for you. Minimizing your visibility and impact at work might affect how people perceive you within the organization's culture, especially if it is important to be perceived as busy, hard working, results-oriented and successful. A key point is to explore the idea of who you are in socio-cultural situations and what effect you have on others and events as they evolve.

There are steps you can take to see how you unknowingly affect the events, processes and relationships at your place of work without harming how you are perceived. Choose an event that you consistently attend such as a family dinner, coffee break at work, a car pool ride with business associates or a workout session with friends. After you have missed the event (due to other priorities, illness, or just to see what does or does not happen a result), ask two or more of the regular attendees who were at the event what stayed the same and what (if anything) was different as a result of you not being there. Do this for two to three events where the majority of the participants are different across groups and events. Reflect on what you learned. What did you learn about your presence or non-presence in different social settings? Did anything you heard surprise you?

Getting Specific

Drawing a sociogram is an advanced skill in seeing yourself and others as a part of the system you are a part of (5). The technique requires you to document your interactions in a setting you are participating in, preferably in real time. An ideal setting to do this in is a meeting.

Begin by sketching out the seating arrangement around the conference table. Then, chart the verbal communication. When an individual initiates a communication, designate it by drawing an arrow with the tip facing the person or persons that the communication was directed to. Then, chart the resulting communications, again with arrows. If it is not possible to do this in real time, draw the sociogram immediately following the meeting. Doing it real time is more accurate than doing so later as your memory fades over time. Do this over several meetings and compare your sociograms to look deeper. Look at Table 5.2.1. The Sociogram (page 108). What patterns do you see?

- What are the titles of the individuals?
- What are the reporting lines?
- Who likes or dislikes one another?
- What are their positions in the informal hierarchy of the group?
- What is the topic that is being discussed?
- What are the ages of the individuals?
- How long have the individuals worked for the company?

- Have there been any recent changes in the reporting relationships?
- Is the organization changing in any way that is relevant to the group and how it communicates?
- Is the group productive?
- What issues/challenges does the group face as this particular time?
- Is there a technical expert in the meeting?
- What would you observe and learn about your role in the meeting if you were Jim? Vicki? Carolyn?

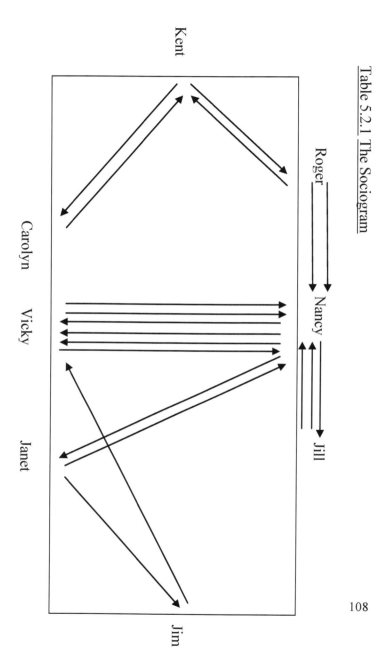

Table 5.2.1 The Sociogram

"Doing anthropological research on one's own 'culture' entails certain difficulties. The very familiarity of the scene diverts attention from important topics, and biases judgment. We probably did our best fieldwork with Indians and Hutterites, both of whom had relatively exotic cultures from the North American viewpoint. Farmers and ranchers, being much more familiar, were perhaps treated less intensively, at least in some sectors of their culture (6)."

John Bennett

"The nimbleness and heartiness that resilient people show in the face of adversity result from an elasticity that allows them to remain relatively calm in unpredictable environments; they can spring back repeatedly after being subjected to the stresses of change. In fact, when resilient people face the ambiguity, anxiety, and loss of control that accompany major change, they tend to grow stronger from their experiences rather than feel depleted by them (7)."

Daryl Connor

This fictionalized account takes place in the Law Department of a large U.S. Firm. Nancy, the General Council, is announcing to the senior legal and administrative staff that she has brought Jill in from outside of the company to be the department's new leader. Jim, the former leader, would take a special but not yet specified position in the department. Nancy brought Vicky (a senior attorney) into the department from a subsidiary four months ago. Kent and Roger are senior attorneys and Janet and Carolyn are senior administrative staff members.

You can also do this at the dinner table at home, the tennis match at the club or in many other settings. The technique helps you view the interaction in a setting and your role in it in a more objective fashion. It also works in situations when you are in contact with a new group and you want to start to understand some of the dynamics of the new group.

A Note on Bias

Research bias is introduced when the researcher is unaware of a particular thought or feeling they have about what they are studying that causes them not to see what is going on clearly. Their thoughts or feelings cause them to interpret what they see in a way that impairs their objectivity.

In anthropological research, the most common culprit is called ethnocentrism. Ethnocentrism is the process of viewing and interpreting an experience from the viewer's cultural orientation and viewing the viewer's culture as better than the other culture.

Once a student wrote a cultural analysis of a local Hispanic merchant area. The area of town was undergoing a renaissance of sorts. Many Hispanic ethnic groups had purchased storefronts in the area and opened businesses such as restaurants, boutiques and folk art stores. When the student described the area, he mentioned that it was noisy and crowded. The words noisy and crowed were interpretations by the observer from his own cultural preferences with his cultural experience used as the metric against which to measure the Hispanic experience. A key to unbiased anthropological research is to first learn how events and processes are interpreted by those from that culture. If asked, someone of Hispanic descent might think of the experience as vibrant.

Ethnocentrism rears its ugly head frequently in business management situations. Think, for example, of a merger situation. The acquiring company's management group often views themselves as better than the management of the firm that they are acquiring. They do this as they usually are the more successful company. And, they use their performance metrics as the points of comparison. The acquired managers respond to the perceived arrogance of the conquering management team with mistrust. So, ethnocentrism is a key problem in cross-cultural situations whether we are in an inner city location or the boardroom. The behavioral dynamics that result from ethnocentric attitudes and behavior can complicate an already complex and difficult situation. At the core is an inability to understand the culture on its own terms before evaluative and judgmental thought and behavioral processes take over. Looking beneath the surface is a preventive skill for those with ethnocentric tendencies.

Notes:

(1) Argyris, Chris and David Schon. <u>Theory in Practice</u>: <u>Increasing Professional Effectiveness</u>. Jossey-Bass, 1974.
(2) Argyris, Chris and David Schon. <u>Organizational Learning</u>: <u>A Theory of Action Perspective</u>. Addison-Wesley, 1978.
(3) Reck, Gregory. <u>In the Shadow of Tlaloc</u>: <u>Life in a Small Mexican Village</u>. Penguin Books, 1978, pp. 39 - 40.
(4) For more information on *Star Trek's* Prime Directive see: <u>http://memory-alpha.org/wiki/Prime Directive</u>, or <u>http://www.youtube.com/watch?v=4mH-L6UCCAE</u>. The Directive states that members of Starfleet are not to interfere in the internal affairs of another species, especially the natural development of pre-warp civilizations, either by direct intervention, or technological revelation. When studying a planet's civilization, particularly during a planetary survey, the Prime Directive makes it clear that there is to be no identification of self or mission. No interference with the social development of said planet. No references to space, other worlds, or advanced civilizations. Starfleet personnel are required to understand that allowing cultures to develop on their own is an important right and therefore must make any sacrifice to protect cultures from contamination, even at the cost of their own lives.
(5) For more information on sociograms, see Scott, John. <u>Social Network Analysis</u>. Sage Publishers, 2000. Scheinker, Jan and Alan Scheinker. <u>Metacognitive Approach to Social Skills Training</u>. Jones and Bartlett, 1988.

(6) Bennett, John. <u>Northern Plainsmen</u>: <u>Adaptive Strategy and Agrarian Life</u>. Aldine, 1969, pp. 4-5.

(7) Connor, Daryl. <u>Managing at the Speed of Change</u>: <u>How Resilient Managers Succeed and Prosper Where Others Fail</u>. Villard Books, 1993, pg. 229.

Another Life Lesson: Lost Luggage

Consistency is the last refuge of the unimaginative.

Oscar Wilde

"Would you like your baggage checked through all the way to Ilheus, Brazil sir?" asked the American Airlines Gate Agent in Minneapolis. Not really paying attention I said, "Yes."

I guess I'd been through the gate check-in procedure so many times that my brain was on automatic pilot. But now, here I am, fourteen hours later in Sao Paulo, Brazil in a panic. I had arrived at ten a.m. today (Sunday morning) in Sao Paulo via Chicago and Miami and had six hours to kill in the Garurya Airport with nothing to do except read, people watch and work on my presentation and workshop until my connecting flight. The topic of my presentation was "Strategic Planning and Core Competencies." I was leading the Monday afternoon part of the annual manager's retreat for a large multinational business management and geographic management team. The discussion would be very stimulating. No one had ever done a geographic strategic plan in Latin America for this company and this was the first step in that direction.

It was now thirty minutes until the departure of my Varig flight north to Ilheus. Twenty-five minutes ago I had awakened from a short reverie realizing that the funny feeling I had in the Minneapolis Airport when I affirmed the agent's question about

115

checking my bags through to Ilheus should have been taken seriously. On international flights all bags must be checked through customs at the first port of entry in the first new country. My bags were not checked through to Ilheus. They were here somewhere in the airport and I needed to find them and recheck them as fast as I could or I would have only a pair of jeans, a golf shirt and running shoes as my clothing for a week on a white-beached island off the coast of northern Brazil in February.

I was returning for the third time from the International to the Domestic side of the Airport terminal, totally frustrated. Luckily the International and Domestic Airport in Sao Paulo are on opposite sides of the oblong building, unlike many of the other airports around the world where they are often miles apart. Once I had realized that I hadn't claimed my luggage five and half-hours ago, I searched the airport for the American Airlines Information Office. I found it located at the top of the stairs on the Domestic side of the concourse. The gentleman behind the desk there told me to go down the stairs, across the concourse, past the taxi desk and through the glass doors to the American Airlines Baggage Office which would be through the second door on the left. I would find my luggage there. I had made the run twice and was sweaty, frustrated and anxious. On the first trip, I followed his directions exactly. When I went through the glass doors I was in a parking lot on the backside of the airport. Looking around I saw no doors, just cars, asphalt and palm trees.

I had just retraced my steps on the second trip, figuring I had rushed and missed something in his directions. Once again I entered the Information Office through its glass door and approached the same American Airlines employee. I asked him the same question as before. He looked at me like I was clueless and said, a little impatiently, "Sir, down the stairs, past the taxi counter, through the double glass doors, second door on the left." Then he returned to his work. So I ran down the stairs, past the taxi desk, through the double glass doors, into the parking lot and stopped because once again, there was no baggage office there. Then I thought to myself, "Between my lousy Portuguese and his pretty good English, there must have been a communication problem." I walked back to the AA Information Office but couldn't go in. I decided to take one more look for myself. As I approached the glass doors to the parking lot, I saw two wooden doors to my left. . "Ah," I thought. "My problems are solved. He must have meant wood when he said glass!" Feeling somewhat relieved and confident, I approached the double wooden doors. I noticed a sign on one door, which said "Restricted Area." Under normal conditions I would never enter a restricted area. But, these were no longer normal circumstances. So, I opened the doors and walked into a typically Brazilian, dimly lit hallway with pale green tile floor and grayish yellow walls. I walked cautiously down the hallway. Upon coming to the second door on my right, I turned the knob only to realize that the door was locked. I knocked repeatedly as this door corresponded to where I thought the second door on the left would be from the outside of the building. No one answered. Feeling disturbed and annoyed I explored the further reaches of the corridor only to find a custodian's closetand an employee break room. There were other doors and other knocks, but no answers. I felt alone and defeated. "I must stop and collect myself, "I thought. "What should I do next?"

I have never been comfortable with defeat. Suddenly my momentary depression and reflective process ended. I turned angry. My adrenaline surged and I became almost frantic as I realized the nearing of my departure time. I have learned over the years to be aware when this surge of anger happens. Unchecked it had and could again make things worse, not better. So, I took another moment to breathe, relax and think. I closed my eyes to hasten the process. Then, I opened my eyes and sprinted back to the American Airlines Information Office in the Domestic Terminal for one, last attempt to find my baggage. As I approached the now familiar office, desk and employee, obviously out of breath, the gentleman looked up as I opened the door and queried, "Sir, your baggage is found?" To which I said, "No." I added, "I think we have mis-communicated. Would you be kind enough to accompany me to find the baggage office? I cannot find it on my own. I have followed your instructions but to no avail." "But sir," he said. "It is easy... Down the stairs, past the..."

At that point I looked him directly in the eye and said, "You must take me there now. I cannot find it on my own." He rolled his eyes, grabbed his keys, walked through his doorway, locked his office door and said sternly, "Follow me!"

As we walked briskly down the terminal stairs he said, "Sir, down the stairs." As we passed the taxi desk he pointed to the taxi desk and said "Past the taxi desk." As we went through the glass doors he said, "Through the glass doors." Then we walked into the parking lot, but we did not stop as I had. We continued walking to the end of the building took a left and walked about twenty more feet. There we found a door labeled "American Airlines Baggage Office." He motioned to the door and said, "Second door on the left. Sir, your luggage should be here." Then he threw up his arms in disbelief and said, "Idiot American!" and walked away, seemingly disgusted.

Opening the door, I found my suitcase and over-the-shoulder bag sitting on the counter. I walked in and said to the lady who was managing the desk, "These are my bags." She said, "Sign here for them." I did and began the mad dash back to the Domestic Terminal to my Varig flight. I arrived five minutes before my departure and was greeted by my friends from the company, Brian, Jay and Hugo.

If only it ended there. More about the two and one half hour bus ride with the broken air conditioner, the transmission problems, the pontoon ride to the island, and the Frugal Gourmet later.

Lessons Learned:

1. Always pay attention to the funny feeling inside, especially when you are tired or on automatic.
2. Don't assume that the other person mis-communicated with you.
3. Don't assume that the baggage office should be accessible from the inside of the terminal. That's how it would happen in

Minneapolis, but Minneapolis is not the center of the Universe.
4. Reflect before acting, especially when you feel yourself entering the panic zone.
5. Never take yourself too seriously, as you are an active part of the cultural system you are interacting with!

5.3. Participant Observation.

You have learned that cultural anthropologists pay attention to the world in a unique way. They do this as a structured part of their training. That training provides them with useful tools to help them gain perspective in cross-cultural situations. Hopefully you are starting to see how these skills are relevant for business leaders. Our next step is to discuss more formally the methodology that has been implied in the discussion and exercises to this point: the how to.

My interest in anthropological research was kindled when I read a basic book by Pertti Pelto on the structure of inquiry (1). The book was framed around a fundamental research question. The primary question of any type of research is how can I find true and useful information about a particular domain of phenomena in our universe? The problem includes two closely related questions. First, what techniques and conditions are necessary for exploration of a given domain? Second, how can I know, with some assurance, what another person means when she asserts a proposition about information, and how can I judge whether I can believe her? If I wanted to find new information about stellar bodies such as black holes and their relationships with their host galaxies I would utilize a telescope to help find the facts. The many different domains of our world require their specialized tools and techniques for gathering information about them. However, in the social sciences, it is different. For example, in the study of social media the significant data might be in form of the types and uses of social media technology. Basic research of this type can be carried out without the use of a special observational or measurement instruments, like a telescope. In general, the social sciences differ from other scientific fields in that primary data gathering is in most cases possible without the aid of highly specialized observational instruments. Most primary data in the social sciences come from three sources: directly observing human behavior, listening to and noting contents of human speech, and examining the products of human behavior.

An untrained person looking into a microscope or telescope learns practically nothing from her use of the powerful instrument. Similarly, a non-specialist presented with usage data on social media types can make little sense of this pile of data. Without some kind of additional experience and information, the novice has no framework and no rules for interpreting what she sees. The novice telescope user needs to acquire a conceptual framework for differentiating various types of cosmic entities such as planets, suns, etc. Cultural observations, similarly, make little or no sense unless the observer has a general conceptual framework for sorting out and organizing behavioral elements.

In behavioral and cultural research, the instrument is the human being. We use our eyes, ears and senses to collect and organize the data. To develop the ability to answer fundamental research questions, leaders must develop a perspective that is research based if they want to really know what is going on in their domain. They also need to be able to refresh their perspective so that the *human* instrument is working at maximum effectiveness.

122

The primary research method used by cultural anthropologists is called *Qualitative Research* or *Ethnography*. Methodology refers to the structure of procedures and rules whereby the scientist extrapolates meaning from the data. A key component of anthropological research is participant observation. Anthropologists watch and record what they see and what they hear from individuals in a particular setting (2). Anthropologists refer to their research as fieldwork, as it doesn't happen in the lab. It happens in the field or the real world. They conduct fieldwork in a cross-cultural setting (a setting which is foreign to them) for an extended period of time (one to two years) as a part of their preliminary training and then t perform their doctoral research. The research process culminates in them writing and defending their doctoral thesis before a committee of experts in their field. The research breaks new theoretical ground and is reviewed and approved (hopefully) by their doctoral committee.

During their research anthropologists attempt to become a part of the every day activities of the community they live in without altering it. They observe and document the physical and natural setting of the community, activities, conversations and physical artifacts relevant to the focus of their study while they observe and participate in the culture. This research process is called participant observation (3, 4, 5). They attempt to develop two levels of insight into the culture through participant observation. The first is the perspective of the "insider." They know they have reached a first, basic level of insight when they know some of the language, which allows them to participate in day-to-day activities. They also begin to understand how individuals understand the culture they participate in and what it means to them. As their time living in the culture increases and they develop more rapport and trust with members of the culture, they are included in more activities not available to "non-locals." They might be invited into a family's home for dinner or included in a religious festival. By participating in these more exclusive cultural activities, their understanding increases. They begin to gain insight into the meaning and significance of the cultural activities in a broader and deeper way. For example, if you were to explore the culture of playing computer games with adolescent boys you would start by playing the most popular games. Next you would talk with adolescent boys who play the games learning the unique jargon of the games and the players. Over time you gain credibility as a player in their minds and mutual trust forms. Perhaps then you are asked to play a particular game with one or more of the boys. By this time you would be able to describe the experience in a fair and accurate fashion. You might even gain some insight into the broader aspects of the culture of adolescent boys. The culture becomes your gym (see Outliers, pages 53-54).

A second level of insight is the "outside" or theoretical perspective. The outside perspective is driven by an attempt to interpret what they are observing and learning as insiders within a broader, more comparative or theoretical context. The larger context gives researchers a point of comparison or interpretation. Following on the computer game example, you would, perhaps, read about the functional aspects of games for children and what they teach and how they are used. You could also read literature on adolescent development. Also, you could read about games that are played by children of a similar age in various cultures around the world, noting the similarities and differences of the games and their functionality within the culture. As a result of this research process you would be better able to discern the cultural aspects of adolescent boys playing computer games from a variety of points of view, adding your unique understanding (theory) of games and their function in adolescent life.

This distinction between the inside and outside view has an age-old pedigree in the social sciences (6). The emic or inside perspective follows in the tradition of psychological studies of folk beliefs and in cultural anthropologists' striving to understand culture from "the native's point of view." The etic or outside perspective follows in the tradition of behavioral psychology and anthropological approaches that link cultural practices to external, antecedent factors, such as economic or ecological conditions, that may not be salient to cultural insiders. Etic and emic approaches traditionally have been associated with differing research methods. Methods in emic research are more likely to involve sustained, wide-ranging observations of a single cultural group. In a business setting, this could be an in-depth analysis of the values and attitudes of financial employees in a company. Methods in etic research are more likely to involve brief, structured observations of several cultural groups. A key feature of etic methods is that observations are made in a parallel manner across differing settings. For instance, matched samples of financial employees in a large multi-national company in many different countries may be surveyed to uncover dimensions of cross-national variation in values and attitudes.

125

While there are arguments for each of these two perspectives as well as combinations of the two in the research literature (7), the novice researcher should stick to learning the emic approach (8). "The emic, or new research approach, emphasizes the importance of collecting data in the form of verbatim texts from native informants in order to preserve the original (i.e. "native") meaning of the information (1, pg. 68)." The danger of beginning with an etic approach is imposing an outside view on a group without understanding the nuances of the culture from the employees' perspective. For example, if one were to read an etic study about values and attitudes of financial employees in international companies, can one be assured that what he reads is relevant to the financial employees of an American, Dutch or Brazilian company? Probably not. It is best to first understand the emic perspective in a company and then to think more theoretically about the values and attitudes of your financial employees in comparison to what researchers have written about more broadly or what you have observed in other companies. As Glasser and Strauss say in their seminal book The Discovery of Grounded Theory:

Generating a theory from data means that most hypotheses and concepts not only come from the data, but are systematically worked out in relation to the data during the course of the research. Generating a theory involves the process of research. By contrast, the source of certain ideas, or even "models" can come from sources other than the data (9, pg. 6).

Many managers want to try the latest fad or something that worked at another organization. These concepts over the years have ranged from quality circles, empowerment, reengineering, leadership competencies, lean manufacturing and business acumen, to name only a few. Bringing trendy business concepts into the corporation and using them to try to change human behavior oftentimes causes problems rather than solving them. These management theories are often implemented without emic research and the development of grounded theory in the challenges that face an organization.

A Business Example

In the 1990's I consulted with the senior managers of a medium-sized local company that was having difficulty retaining its key managers. The company was in a segment of the information technology industry. In an attempt to improve the retention of middle managers, senior management created a series of seminars for employees who exhibited high potential as managers. The senior managers had participated in similar high potential management development seminars in the companies they worked in prior to joining the current company.

They reasoned that if the company demonstrated that it was interested in the employees for long-term employment by offering the developmental seminars, the employees would feel a part of the firm's future and choose to stay. Both the company and the individuals would benefit from the new skills acquired. The seminars were developed, delivered and attended. Attendees

From an informal interview with a self-proclaimed generation x employee...

"I am Denise of the generation we like to call Generation neXt... grew up under the red scare, nuclear war and that there would be no personal economic security. In effect, my generation was given the message to work hard, make as much money as you can in the shortest period of time, and hope like heck the world is still here for you to enjoy. The resulting effect is an entire generation of people whose priority it is to work hard and play hard at the same time while storing away as much money as possible through the fastest growing financial plans while still living paycheck to paycheck. Oh yeah, and we want to work at jobs that are cool and for a good company. Otherwise we'll find another place. By the time I'm fifty, I should have not one pension but two and enough money stored away in my 401 K to sustain me though my senior years—providing that I quit working at fifty. If I have children great, if not, oh well, life goes on. Having a family is important but not a priority. Ensuring my economic welfare is. These beliefs permeate through Generation next (10)."

evaluated the seminars very positively. But, more key manager turnover ensued.

The senior managers were completely dumbfounded! What had worked years before in large, international companies like GE and IBM that they had come from was not working here. A problem was that the senior managers were limited by using only their outside or etic perspectives. By outside, I mean views based on their business experience including the knowledge and experience from the large, international companies they had worked for. They had not fully realized what it meant to have a negative unemployment rate for managers of information technology companies, as that was a new phenomenon of the late 1990's. Their experience was based in an earlier economy of significant unemployment. Negative unemployment was also a dilemma between and among smaller, emerging information technology companies in their geographical area. The senior managers had all grown up in a time when some percentage of unemployment was the norm. However, at this time, there were more jobs than workers. In addition, many of their high potential employees were Generation X workers who were more interested in sharpening their skills and moving from company to company seeking to work on the best projects than developing a loyalty to one or two employers for their entire career. The courses made the employees more marketable in their field rather than building loyalty. The actions of the senior managers actually made the situation worse, not better for their company. The senior managers should have spent time trying to understand the

"What is big and emerging in countries like China and India is a new consumer base consisting of hundreds of millions of people. Starved for choice for over 40 years, the rising middle class is hungry for consumer goods and a better quality of life and is ready to spend... When managers in the West hear about the emerging middle class of India or China, they tend to think in terms of the middle class in Europe or the United States. This is one sign of an imperialist mindset; the assumption that everyone must be like 'us.' True, consumers in the emerging markets today are much more affluent than they were before their countries liberalized trade, but they are not affluent by Western standards. This is usually the first mistake that multinational companies (MNCs) make (11)."

Prahalad, C.K., and Kenneth Lieberthal

motivation and aspirations of their high potential managers rather than relying only on their theoretical knowledge about employee motivation and aspiration from their historical experiences. Once this point was made and explained, the senior managers created employee forums where they held discussions with employees about the employees' motivation and career aspirations.

They formed new insights derived from the data from the discussions and viewed the situation through the eyes of the employees in the company and in the leadership development program. Now, enabled by their learning experience, the senior managers are attempting to attract and retain managers by accentuating the work itself, the innovative nature of the work processes of the company and investing in employee development. Turnover has slowed as a result of viewing the problematic situation from a perspective that was based in the current experience of their employees and the resulting reframing of the issues.

Leading with an Anthropological Mindset

The goal of the anthropologist is to gain the inside (emic) insight to develop better understanding and create better theory and decisions based on actual human experience and grounded research. For most business managers, the goal is the same. However, they tend to work with their larger, theory-based perspectives on management, customer service, etc. without the benefit of grounded research. Our business schools often work with a cookie cutter approach to curriculum, teaching the established body of knowledge, discipline by discipline, without teaching their students how to collect data and perform fieldwork-based research. They teach theorists' models of organization, human behavior and customer and community experience without cautioning the students to consider the fit or relevance of the theory to the actual situation.

Business managers who grew up in a business are insiders to their business cultures. They have a different problem. They must attempt to gain the outside perspective on their culture to accentuate a point of separation and comparison. They need to find a way to the balcony to look freshly at their organization. They must also learn to conduct comparative analysis between their organization and others. Finally, they can then reenter their organization figuratively to look beneath the surface and see more accurately the emic nature of the organization.

Leading with an anthropological mindset means recognizing both emic and etic assumptions and approaches and conducting actual grounded research to probe issues and develop theories to use in their mitigation. The tendency toward the quick fix mentality using a borrowed theory or someone's bright idea should be recognized and rejected as a business leadership process.

New and Experienced Employees

The following exercise will help you gain a greater develop both an inside and an outside perspective. Interview new employees who have been with your firm for less than six months. The employees will have perceptions of the culture of your firm from an outside perspective, as they probably have not yet been totally enculturated into the culture of your firm. You can interview individuals singly or in groups of five to seven. Begin by getting an informal feel to the conversations, especially if you are a senior manager. Position talks! To make the meeting less formal have a luncheon, supply snacks and an informal setting like a round table. Set a ground rule that there are no sacred cows or taboo subjects to talk about. You are their strictly to learn. Ask them about what they think about the company and its products or services. Ask about their general experience in your company and then move on to more specific questions. For example, ask them if they have found anything unusual about your company in comparison to others they have worked for. How do they define what success is for your company? What do they see as the company's greatest positive and negative aspects? A great discussion starter is "What are the informal rules around here?" Listen carefully and take notes. Try to keep yourself from becoming defensive, wanting to disagree with a point or trying to explain why certain things are as they are. Are there any patterns in what the individuals have said? Record your observations.

Have these informal discussions with new employees frequently. They will help you discover some of the key features of your organization's culture as perceived by fresh eyes and minds. Hold similar meetings with customers, suppliers and other external stakeholders to further enrich your perspective.

Interview employees who have been with the company for a long time, say 10 years or more. The employees will have perceptions of the culture of your firm from an inside perspective, as they have likely been totally enculturated into the culture of your firm. Ask them about their perceptions of the company and its products or services before they joined. Ask about their general experience in your company and then move on to more specific questions. For example, ask them if they have found anything unusual about your company in comparison to others they have worked for. How do they define what success is for your company? What do they see as the company's greatest positive and negative aspects? And a great discussion starter is "What are the informal rules around here?" Listen carefully and take notes. Try to keep yourself from becoming defensive, wanting to disagree with a point or trying to explain why certain things are as they are. Are there any patterns in what the individuals have said? Record your observations.

Have these informal discussions with experienced employees frequently. They will help you discover some of the key features of your organization's culture as perceived by employees with years of cultural experience at your firm. Hold similar meetings with customers, suppliers and other external stakeholders to enrich further your perspective.

Compare and contrast what you observe and hear during these discussions. They will help you learn to see your organization from different points of view.

Advanced Participant Observation

Think of your favorite T.V. private investigator from vintage television. I saw a list a few months back in the local newspaper ranking them from best to worst. Remember these shows: *Kojak, The Rockford Files, Magnum P.I., Columbo, Murder, She Wrote* and *Barnaby Jones*? Or, think about current shows such as *CSI, Monk* or *Burn Notice*. What are the skill sets the investigators have in common? Five follow:

1. Observing and interacting with people to collect information.
2. Finding and interpreting clues, leading them to the truth in the process
3. Having an open and inquisitive mind.
4. Not being easily fooled.
5. Capable of working through contradictory information.

These skill sets are very similar to the participant observations skills that anthropologists employ. A major difference is that while P.I.'s are trying to discover the truth and catch the bad guy, anthropologists are attempting to understand and interpret the concept of culture in different socio-cultural situations. For both there is a continuum of the degree of interaction from pure observation to structured, formal interviewing that they use as a part of their methodology. A summary of the different types of participant observation methods appears on the next page.

Exercise

To gain a better understanding of the progression of participant observation skills, complete the following exercise.

1. Pure Observation. Choose a social setting that is unfamiliar such as a musical concert. Attend a concert that is new and unusual to you. Start by observing the people and activities from a distance. Arrive early and choose an observation post. Make sure to dress in a way that will make you look similar to others at the concert. If possible, take notes and create a drawing of the physical setting and any other important aspects of the concert.

2. Participant Observation. Move from pure observation to participant observation. Become a part of the crowd. Get in line with other concert- goers and buy a refreshment. Walk around experiencing other sights and sounds. If possible, record your thoughts, feelings and other experiences.

3. Informal Interviewing. During the concert get into the behavior appropriate to the culture. If it is a chamber group smile and applaud politely. If it is a Lady Gaga concert, well, get loud. Begin to interact with those around you. For example, while applauding politely exchange smiles with those around you or get up on your chair and dance whatever is culturally appropriate. During a break in the performance whether between songs are at a formal

break, interact with those near you in a more deliberate way. Ask questions such as, "Are you enjoying the concert?" If your question is warmly received, venture a bit further. Ask about the person's experience. For example, ask "What aspects are you enjoying most or least?" Your goal is to elicit from the person or persons their sense of important aspects of the concert experience and their meaning and significance to the individual. If you are feeling very adventurous mingle a little further from your seat.

4. Formal Interviews. Review your experience at the concert. Go over your notes. What questions come to mind that would help you better understand the concert culture from the participant's view? From the promotional group's view? From the view of the musical group? From the venue management's view? Schedule a follow up interview with one or more of these parties. Create your interview questions based on your thoughts. Conduct the interview(s).

5. Reflect on what you learned about the concert culture.

6. What did you learn about participant observation?

7. What did you learn about yourself and your perspective?

Table 5.3.1 Types and Uses of Participant Observation Techniques

	Pure Observation	Participant Observation	Informal Interviewing	Structured Interviewing
Concept	Watching cultural activity without interacting, usually from an observation point on the periphery of the setting. Also includes reading cultural material and observing artifacts.	Joining in the cultural activities in order to experience the culture but to ensure that the researcher does not disrupt the activities because of his/her presences.	Talking with individuals in the cultural setting while being a participant observer. The interviews are informal because they happen as a natural part of the activities.	The interviewer prepares a set of questions for a cultural participant. The responses to the questions are carefully recorded.

Table 5.3.1 Types and Uses of Participant Observation Techniques (Continued)

	Pure Observation	Participant Observation	Informal Interviewing	Structured Interviewing
When to use/ When not to use	When it is difficult to gain access to the cultural activities, when the researcher needs to maintain anonymity or when the researcher is concerned about affecting cultural activities. Be careful not to observe cultural activities the host culture wo not approve of, such as certain religious activiti or a confidential business meeting.	When you can gain access to the cultural activities and you want to experience them fully. This also leads to developing relationships with individuals within the culture. These individuals can help the researcher understand the meaning and significance of cultural activities.	Informal interviewing is best used in casual cultural contact as part of broader participant observation research. The researcher should be careful not to introduce new cultural information. Rather, she should ask questions that are within the culture in an attempt to better understand.	When you have already conducted less formal cultural analysis techniques to explore specific questions. Also use when it is difficult to get access to cultural activities but insiders are willing to be interviewed about cultural activities.

139

A Note on Informal Interviewing in a Cultural Context

Interviewing to collect cultural information takes practice. The key is to ask open-ended questions in a casual manner. An open-ended question is a question that allows the person that is asked the question to elaborate with and on their own terms. This is opposed to closed questions for which the answer is a yes, no or another conversation limiting answer. Of course some individuals who do not wish to be bothered will answer an open-ended question with a simple answer to let you know that they are not interested in your question.

Open-ended questions:

- Please tell me about yourself.
- What are some of your favorite experiences?
- How does this operate?
- Please help me understand what is happening here.

Closed questions:

- What is your name?
- How old are you?
- Do you like this musical group?
- What do you do for work?

Sometimes it is important to start a conversation with a closed question. For example, it is a custom in many situations to introduce yourself and ask the other person to introduce himself. However, the researcher's goal is to learn about the cultural experience of the person being interviewed. After introductory formalities is the time to ask some more open-ended questions. Asking open questions jump-starts the communications process. As the interviewed person talks, he provides the researcher with content clues: words and phrases to follow up on. The following example will illustrate the process.

The interviewer asks, "Please tell me a little bit more about yourself."

The person interviewed says, "I'm twenty-four, female and I live in the downtown area. I like to run around the lakes and read. And, I'm single but involved."

Content clues are words or phrases the person being interviewed uses in their answer. The content clues are *twenty-two, female, lives downtown, likes running around the lakes, likes to read, is single and involved*. These are clues to further areas of interest and concern to the person being interviewed. The interviewer follows by asking another open question exploring areas of information labeled by the content clues. What is living downtown like? Be careful to choose areas to ask further question in that are not invasive. For example, it is probably wise to follow up with "What is it like to live downtown?" rather than "What does it mean to be twenty-four and single but involved?" Build trust with the person you interview. It starts with easy questions that put the person at ease.

The follow up question can lead to more clues for further exploration. Perhaps she *lives downtown* because of the proximity to theatre. ("What plays have you enjoyed lately?") In a complete interview, the researcher would track each of the content clues asking open-ended questions about each clue at each point in the conversation, going deeper in areas that the person being interviewed (the informant, to anthropologists) is more willing to elaborate about. The depth of the interview will depend on the length and quality of the relationship with the person. A complete interview will have covered some or many of the content clues and their subsequent content clues so the researcher can begin to get a better understanding of the person and her experience. More familiarity and trust

"Oh. I get it now. Ethnographic research is like deep hanging out."

An MBA student

will yield lengthier discussions with deeper insights into the person and her experience. Don't push to go deeper than the person is comfortable with. Take your time to develop the relationship. You really know someone and their cultural experience when you can anticipate much of how they reflect on and interpret their experience.

This technique takes practice. Begin to practice as you have contact with interesting people in your everyday life such as at the local hardware store. Ask the proprietor about his business. "How's business?" Or, at the local deli begin a conversation with the baker about the breads. "I love your breads. Can you tell me about them?" How about the bagger at the grocery store? "What's the life of a bagger like?" Little by little, as your comfort grows, push the conversations a little further.

Conduct an informal interview with someone. Reflect on the informal interview content clues. Now go through the rest of the conversation you had. What follow up questions did you ask for the content clues that were answered by the person interviewed? Were the follow up questions successful in getting the person to talk about the content clue? Did you cover most of the areas? Why or why not? What did you learn? What would you do differently next time? The next time you conduct an informal interview remember what you learned previously and incorporate it into the next informal interview. You will be awed and inspired by how much people like to talk about themselves and the things that are important and significant to them!

Leaders and those in the process of becoming leaders not only need to look beneath the surface and realize that they are a part of the system they are participating in. They need to develop their qualitative/ethnographic research skills. They cannot depend completely on their prior experience or theories from a management text or a consultant to tell them what to do. They need to develop their own appreciation of their domain by interacting and studying their organization and its related systems, such as employees and customers. They must develop their own theories that are grounded in their company. By developing this skill, they can constantly see their company anew and develop and refresh their leadership perspective.

Notes:

(1) Pelto, Pertti. Anthropological Reasearch: The Structure of Inquiry. Harper & Row, 1970.
(2) Berg, Bruce. Qualitative Research Methods for the Social Sciences (7th Edition). Allyn and Bacon, 2005.
(3) Fetterman, David. Ethnography: Step-by-Step (Applied Social Research Methods.) Sage, 2010.
(4) Fick, Uwe. An Introduction to Qualitative Research. Sage, 2002.
(5) Madison, D. Soyini. Critical Ethnography. Sage, 2005.
(6) Pike, Kenneth. Language in Relation to a Unified Theory of the Structure of Human Behavior. Mouton, 1967.
(7) Morris , Michael, Kwo Leung, Daniel Ames and Brian Licke. *Views from Inside and Outside: Integrating Emic and Etic Insights about Culture and Justice Judgment*. Academy of Management Review, 1999, Vol. 24. No. 1, 781-796.
(8) Locke, Karen. Grounded Theory in Management Research. Sage, 2001.
(9) Glaser, Barney and Anselm Strauss. The Discovery of Grounded Theory: Strategies for Qualitative Research. Aldine, 1967.
(10) For more information on generational issues see, Cummins, H.J. *Generations Collide.* Minneapolis StarTribune, Section D, pp. 1-4, Sunday, November 27, 2005.
(11) Prahald, C.K. and Kenneth Lieberthal. "The End of Corporate Imperialism." *Harvard Business Review*, July-August, 1998, pg. 71.

Accountants Go Native

Adventure travel is not for the faint of heart.

Albi Daniels

I couldn't believe it! "What the hell is that? Oh no! What should I do?" I blurted out loud.

It seemed so innocent yet adventuresome at the same time. "One half day rain forest jungle trek with guide. Be sure to bring or wear your bathing costume" read the advertisement in the Sheraton Langkawi brochure. Five of us had a half day to burn before we caught our flight back to Singapore and then back to the States. We had participated for three days in the first ever Asia Pacific Sector Financial Managers' meetings in Langkawi, Malaysia. Langkawi is a resort island in the far northern part of Malaysia. You can see Thailand in the distance.

Actually, I think it was Karen's idea. We were five corporate citizens who just happened to be standing in the lobby of the hotel at the same time. I was thinking of golf, Jim was thinking of doing some work and Arlan was going to hang out by the pool. "Oh, come on you guys," she said, "Don't think like accountants. Let's get out of the box and do something unusual and fun." So we did.

Forty-five minutes later we were in a van with a driver and guide on our way to the trail. We were dropped off at what looked like a park at the base of a mountain range. There were two grass covered buildings and a crushed stone parking lot. One building sold snacks and the other had shirts and skirts. We were the only hikers there.

The initial climb was uneventful, but a lot of work. It reminded me of the old University of Minnesota Memorial Stadium steps that I used to run to get in shape when I was in graduate school. There were sixty-three steps from the field up to the nosebleed section and they got steeper as you got higher. The highest was a full twenty inches. I remember the stadium record was twenty-nine minutes for a complete trip around the stadium up and down every set of stairs. A major difference was that this was now and it was forty minutes of non-stop, twenty inch, cement step climbing in the jungle of Northern Malaysia. Along side our path was what looked like a large water pipe. It was approximately forty-eight inches in diameter and was made of steel. The steps must have been for maintenance workers. It was hot and humid—ninety-five degrees Fahrenheit with humidity of seventy-five percent or more.

Dripping wet, twenty-five minutes after beginning, we reached the first stop, a pool where rain and river water collected to feed the water pipe. Looking down we saw the rain forest. Looking up through the jungle mist we could see the mountain peaks in the distance. After pausing for a few minutes, we rebooted our adventure. Now the story gets good. Read on.

"No more steps," Arlan chortled. He had the bad knees. "Now we can really trek in the jungle." The path was narrow at first alongside the stream and it was too muddy for our liking. We crossed the stream by stepping on stones in the river to keep us dry. Then we saw the monkeys. Perhaps fifteen or twenty of them approached to check us out. Little gray furry things with pink faces. The leader came close and perched on a tree branch a few meters ahead. "A Kodak moment," someone said. We all laughed and reached for our cameras only to have our guide say "Pictures okay, but don't look monkey in the eye. They bite." "The brochure for the jungle trek didn't say anything about biting monkeys," Karen said. Another pause. "Did everyone see the movie *Outbreak* on the plane on the way over here?" someone asked. More laughs ensued. But our laughter wasn't as hearty or genuine as it was a few moments before. I could feel the fear in the group. My heart was pounding signaling my own discomfort with the "cute" monkeys.

Cautiously, we made our way around them and followed the muddy trail along the stream. After a few escapades climbing up small hills and sliding down and then figuring out how to use the vines and trees as aides, we reached our second stop. Now we were not only sweaty and tired, we also were muddy. Above us was a breathtaking waterfall, twenty-five meters or so below was another. Now we saw our destination, a series of small Jacuzzi-like pools. This is what we all had in mind a few hours ago. The view was spectacular! And, we were to play in the water to cool off. A few minutes later we were there. Except for Jim. He had been complaining about something for the last ten minutes and now I could see what he was concerned about. A few small leeches had hold of his ankle and one had drawn a little blood. "The advertisement didn't mention biting monkeys or leaf leeches." He laughed as he plucked them off.

The water was great, cold and clear. It contained small red and green fish that could be seen below the surface. We tried to catch them but they were way too fast for us. It was like swimming in a very large aquarium. We talked, we splashed and we found small places between the rocks where the river rushed through. We sat and let the water relax our tired bodies.

Thirty minutes of relaxation ended with our guide lighting a cigarette and saying, "Time to go. The bus will pick us up soon." The walk down the mountain was easier and faster than the trek up, except for a few minutes of concern. As we passed the area just above where the water collection pond was, we came across two shirtless men, one carrying a large walking stick and the other a machete. They started walking along with us and opened a conversation with Arlan by asking, "You from here?" to which Arlan stated, "No." "Oh, you are American?" they asked. "Yes, I am." "Where in the U.S. do you live? "I don't live in the U.S. I live in Bangkok," Arlan replied. What do you do for work?" they continued. "I am retired." Arlan said. Then the man with the machete summarized the brief conversation with, "Oh, you are retired, rich American living in Thailand." He raised the machete and rested it on his shoulder. He smiled as if he had come across some great idea. Arlan ended the conversation by double-timing his walk.

After a few minutes, to our relief, the two men stopped walking with us. Once we put some distance between them we stopped for a needed breather and talked about our encounter. Once our fear had passed we all had a great laugh. "They didn't have this on the brochure either." Jim stated. I said, "Minneapolis *StarTribune* carries story: 'Four Executives and Consultant Missing in the Jungles of Malaysia'." The gentle walk in the park had been a memorable experience for all of us, binding our friendship and collegiality.

About an hour later I was back in the hotel. That's when it happened. As I took off my sweat drenched clothing, I noticed a leech the size of my thumb beside my foot on the floor of the bathroom. Being a bit squeamish of such critters, I walked a few feet away to the sink to get a tissue to pick it up and flush it back to a more leechy place. As I reached for the tissue, I noticed in the bathroom mirror blood dripping down my left arm from a place on my left shoulder.

I couldn't believe it! That leech had been attached to me for approximately ninety minutes. It must have crawled (or whatever leeches do) into my shirt while we swam in the pool beneath the waterfall. Yew! After disposing of the yucky interloper and showering, my shoulder continued to bleed, not heavily, but a drip every thirty seconds or so. To stop it, I had to be creative as I had no Band-Aids. Kleenex and masking tape did the trick. A short time later, I joined the group back in the lobby where we were to wait for the shuttle to the airport. Karen, Jim and Arlan were

149

recounting our story to other accountants when I approached. As the group looked on in disbelief, I rolled up the sleeve of my shirt exposing the Kleenex and masking tape. The accountants looking on couldn't believe it. Any what's more, they couldn't understand why we were all laughing about it; the monkeys, the swim, the mud, sweat and leeches and the two guys on the path.

It's nice to have the story of the jungle trek told by my friends and colleagues, especially having it be so over the top with the leech ending. The story and its telling will no doubt become a part of the history and culture of the group as it continues its quest to become active, committed and courageous.

With change spiraling around and through us, we must take two notes. First, we cannot change without becoming a part of and experiencing new activities, thoughts, and emotions. Secondly, we must ponder about how relationships are formed and deepened. It could have happened for us by the pool with a beer, I guess. But adventure, danger, success, memories and stories seem to have connected us at a deeper level.

Having a permanent little indentation on your left shoulder the size of a ballpoint pen tip as a memento helps too!

Lessons Learned:

1. See yourself through the eyes of other to get another spin.
2. Seek out new environments to observe, experience and learn.

3. Observe as you participate. Your life might be on the line.
4. The world is a jungle out there. Be prepared for it!

5.4. Theoretical Sampling.

A frequent complaint I hear from senior executives is that they feel that the information they receive in their firms is filtered. I've heard this from CEO's of companies from thirty-three to more than 80,000 employees. When executives travel outside of their corporate offices to a plant location, for example, special plant tours are set up for them, power point presentations are made and welcome dinners are held. Even leaders of very small firms complain that they move from meeting to meeting, gleaning bits of insight from data that has been analyzed and reanalyzed to make sure it is succinct and able to be presented efficiently in twenty minutes or less. One sarcastic leader confided to me that, "Many of the presentations I hear have already been filtered through layers of agenda that represent an emerging or entrenched political coalition's next move, then sanitized so that it passes the executive's sniff test." The same leader stated further, "Or, perhaps the ideas have been filtered through conceptual or pragmatic lenses that are naïve to the company's emerging strategy. Whatever the case, the key word is *filtered*. So, I'm never quite sure that I should trust what I hear because I am so far removed from the actual data and the lenses that examine it."

In many large multi-national companies, executives have so many things to pay attention to and be involved in that they rarely have time to drill down in to the data and architecture of an issue, much less see through the political aspects of data, information and the political and symbolic ramifications of key, strategic decisions. Executives have told me that they often spend as little as two to five minutes on an issue or question before needing to move on to the next. In an early and exhaustive study of the literature on what managers actually do, Colin Hales (1) makes it clear that the executive's world is large, complex and ever changing. While some leaders rise above the fray, other leaders' worlds can become fragmented, technical, reactive and frenetic, leaving them working without appropriate information or a clear agenda. Just imagine what the world of the executive is like twenty-six years after this study was performed?

It is healthy for executives to question the information they receive. What worries me is that it often does not occur to many executives that their information is formed into concepts for them by staff and analysts. They need to do their own homework on an issue or question otherwise they run the risk of being isolated in their ivory towers and pawns in their own organizations.

Theoretical sampling is the process of collecting data for generating theory whereby the person collects and analyzes her data and decides what data to collect next and where to find it, in order to develop her theory as it emerges (2). The social scientist often begins research with a partial framework of concepts that define some of the larger features of the structure, process or people in a situation. For example, she knows before studying a hospital that there will be doctors, nurses, aides, patients, department structures such as emergency or surgery and admissions procedures. These concepts give her a beginning foothold on her research. Of course, she does not know the relevancy of these concepts to her problem – the problem must emerge – nor are they likely to become part of the core explanatory categories of the theory. As she enters the situation she learns more about these categories and start to piece them together into a coherent conceptual or theoretical system (3).

The business manager enters situations like this frequently. However, rather than approaching these situations as an opportunity to learn, managers often enter these situations with an already developed idea of what is going on there and what the problem is, focusing on solving the issue rather than verifying what the issue really is. Outside ideas from other situations she has encountered or from staffers fill her thoughts. The manager must develop her own understanding of what is going on rather than depending solely on the analysis of her staff. She should treat

> *"It is easy to talk about thinking and behaving 'out of the box.' It is far more difficult to actually do it rather than to merely talk about it. Many executives in my company, in other words, talk the talk but they don't walk the walk. That is why our business is in deep trouble competitively. These guys can't even describe the box they are in much less get out of it. And that is why, I'm sorry to say, that their leadership credibility is waning in my eyes."*
>
> Tim, corporate controller

staff ideas and ideas she has from other situations as a partial beginning framework. She should test the preconceived notions she has and develop her own theory as situational features arise.

Theoretical sampling for the business leader is the process of ensuring that (a) she is hearing from points of view other than those in the main stream in her firm and in her life, and (b) that she is seeing phenomena in their pure form, before they have been analyzed and conceptualized by others. This will help give her fresh data for thinking and conceptualizing. As a result of this process she will become more aware of the bias and orthodoxies inherent in her thinking, the thinking of her staff analysts and in her firm's culture. She will become more open to new ideas and perspectives and more capable of developing her own.

Fight Isolation through Establishing Listening Posts

Some executives take conscious steps to ensure that they are not isolated from new and unique ideas, events and people. They sample theoretical points of reality in order to get views which may be different than theirs. A strategic planning executive in a health care company, for example, has set up several "listening posts" in his hospitals. He meets with new employees bi-monthly to dialogue about whatever is on their minds. He is attempting to understand better the needs of his diverse workers and their views of healthcare and work in general. The CEO of a large insurance company meets quarterly with each of the formal special interest groups in his company to understand better their unique ideas and concerns e.g., physically disabled, gay, lesbian,

"No other predator employs as many hunting strategies with one animal than the polar bear does with the ringed seal. It may take a half-hour to patiently approach a seal resting on the edge of an ice flow, surfacing quietly to reconnoiter, then submerging again. A bear may drift toward a seal like an innocent piece of ice. When it stalks seals over the ice, it flattens itself on its forequarters and slides along slowly on chest and forelegs. It will scrape away the sea ice at a breathing hole until there is just a thin layer left, and then cover the ice with its body to cut off sunlight, so it looks to the seal below as if the thick crust of ice and snow is still present. And it will rise up suddenly in a resting seal's own aglu (4)."

Barry Lopez

bisexual and transgender employees, African American employees, female employees, Hispanic employees, etc. A group of senior financial managers at a large international company are visiting other companies in and out of their industry to attempt to gain a perspective on the best practices of financial management including selection, structure, role, job design, promotion, work processes and performance management. They are consciously choosing companies that are smaller and outside of their industry to challenge the orthodoxies of their company's and industry's cultural thought patterns and behavioral practices. They have also noted that they have a big company bias and are trying to fight it.

The process of theoretical sampling ensures that you will hear different points of view, can drill down into an issue and, as a result, are more grounded in the real world of your business. Theoretical sampling provides the leader with fresh ideas to continually learn and develop ideas about business.

Managing the News

Whether we are having our in-laws to dinner, the parents to the school, the executive to the plant or the board of directors to the annual meeting, we all present things in the best light possible. We control access to things, events and people through creating perceptual filters for others to see us through. We steer our visitors away from the things we do not want them to see and toward those people and things that show us in the best light. For example, a guest policy at our home is "no tours of the upstairs." We do this because our children's rooms might be messy. We (the parents) sometimes also are behind on folding and putting away our laundry. We limit access to these rooms because we want our guests to view us as a clean, orderly, professional family, and to prevent them from seeing us as we really are... fairly typical.

In business this game can go too far and become a dangerous practice as executives are consistently presented with a view which may differ from the real view. Managers in one company, for example, use the phrase "managing the news" to refer to the practice of shading reality from senior executives. The purpose of the activity is twofold, first, to keep executives happy by supplying only good news, and second, to prevent executives from knowing enough to want to intervene and begin micro-managing the operation. Of course this seems harmless to the employees who operate in this way... unless a significant problem occurs. Then all hell breaks loose as executives realize they have been purposefully isolated. Once they realize they have been deceived, they pay closer attention to the guilty business managers, which makes the operation more careful with what it divulges. It becomes a vicious, dangerous cycle.

It works a little differently in another of my client organizations in the health and fitness industry. Executives actually stand up to difficult situations when meeting with their CEO. They take the risk and tell the truth as they see it. Sometimes this leads to some animated discussion and debate. But, usually the result is a better understanding of various points of view and an increase in honesty, respect and trust. I guess it helps you voice an unpopular opinion when you can bench press a bus!

"The final and, perhaps, most difficult aspect of the analysis of assumptions has to do with the degree to which they come to be interlocked into paradigms or coherent patterns. Not all assumptions are mutually compatible or consistent with each other. If there is a cognitive drive for order and consistency in the human brain, we can assume that human groups will gradually learn sets of assumptions that are compatible and consistent. If we observe inconsistency and lack of order, we can assume that we are dealing with an as yet unformed culture or that we are observing a conflict among several cultures (5)."

Edgar Schein

"The distinguishing mark of anthropology among the social sciences is that it includes for serious study other societies than our own. [The anthropologist] is interested in the great gamut of custom that is found in various cultures, and the object is to understand the way in which these cultures change and differentiate, the different forms through which they express themselves, and the manner in which the customs of any peoples function in the lives of the individuals who compose them (6)."

Ruth Benedict

Managers need to be aware of their isolation. They need from time to time, to participate in the structuring of problem solving activities, data collection processes and other activities that give them a knowledge of the whole chain of events in a work process. Being isolated might also mean out of touch! Being out of touch in the managerial ranks is a high-risk activity. The following exercise was developed based on the examples and concerns outlined above. The exercise will help you develop best practices for improving learning in your company through this technique.

Exercise: Unscheduled Visits

If you feel isolated from reality and feel the need to get a view of how things really are, make an unscheduled visit to a plant, office location or department in your company. Ask employees about their work, the equipment they use, their productivity and how much they know about the strategy of the company. Record their comments. Are they similar to or different than what you would have heard in an announced visit? Why? Listen carefully to their points of view. Record your thoughts here.

Diversify the Inputs to Your Thinking Process

Another way to increase your perspective is to sample different types of information than you normally do. If you typically read American business publications, for example, read a non-U.S. publication such as *The Economist*. *The Economist* is published in the U.K. and contains overviews of business news in every region of the planet including the U.S. Or, be even a little more adventuresome. On your next business flight, pick up a few magazines that articulate cultural life outside of your experience. A teaching colleague sets out "unusual" magazines on a table in the back of her classroom. The magazines include *The Utne Reader, Rap Music, Violet, Biker Magazine, Ebony, Water Gardens, Tattoo, Cigar Aficionado, Scientific American, This Old House, Heavy Metal, Vanity Fair, Cosmopolitan, Rolling Stone* and others. She watches to see how business students react to the magazines. They usually act coolly at first as if to say, "What are these magazines doing in an Executive MBA classroom?" which is symptomatic of the narrow perspective of some business leaders. Then she gives the following assignment. She asks them as individuals or as a team to juxtapose ideas from two or more magazines and come up with a new business idea. She offers Caribou Coffee certificates as a prize. Here is a list of recent winners:

- Single use, biodegradable hairnets.
- Genetically altered Koi to survive in northern climate water gardens.
- Designer cigars marketed especially for women.

This process is more important than the actual product suggestions. Business students feel silly at first looking at the magazines and then trying to combine disparate ideas together. When asked if this process would be acceptable, with some modification at work, they sheepishly say, "No." When asked to elaborate, students talk about their workplaces as stuffy task-oriented places where divergent and fun activities are not allowed. Magazines like this are taboo. Then my teaching partner asks," How can new ideas be developed by stale processes?" Then the students get the point being made.

Try entertainment venues that are outside your norm. Look through the entertainment section of your local newspaper for unusual (to you) types of entertainment. Try one or more of these:

- A Native American Powwow.
- A small town street fair.
- A professional wrestling match.
- A surrealistic art show.
- A poetry reading.
- A foreign film festival.
- A monster truck show.

When meeting with your business colleagues do something a little different. I find it interesting that many business leaders attempt to "get out of the box" (be creative) yet they plan their business meeting in the same old way. Oftentimes this includes a hotel, conference center or resort as the location. The meeting agenda then includes presentations, discussions and is followed by golf and an elegant dinner. Changing the setting can stimulate new ideas for groups. Try one of these locations:

- A dude ranch.
- A campout in a national forest.
- A sailing trip.

- Kennedy Space Center.
- At a university campus, sleeping in dorm rooms.
- A community center.
- A religious retreat center.
- A historic hotel in a small town.

I planned and facilitated a two day meeting with the senior executives of a $2 billion dollar manufacturing company that was attempting to think longer, more broadly and more creatively about their future. Here is a comparison of their usual planning meeting schedule versus the one we had(See next page). The result of the two-day meeting was the beginnings of a strategic plan that had heightened elements of creativity, a longer time frame and a much more aggressive stance toward the current competitive orthodoxies in their industry.

Another benefit of the meeting was a realization by the senior managers that in order to compete in the future that they would need to experiment with new ideas and behaviors. As one said, "We learned that we can't be spectators. We have to become risk takers and get into the game."

Here are a few other ideas to see a slightly different sample of the world around you to get you out of your normal routine:

- When you drive to work, take all side streets rather than the freeway.
- Listen to a different music station.

Table 5.4.1. The Usual Meeting Design and New Meeting Design

	Usual	New Design
Location	Suburban Chicago hotel.	Historic hotel in downtown Chicago's Gold Coast.
Meeting Design	PowerPoint presentations.	Challenges, large and small group brainstorming and small discussions.
Dinner	Steaks and baked potatoes at a traditional steak and chops shop.	Vietnamese French fusion at a trendy upscale bistro.
Entertainment	Hotel bar.	Tap Dogs performance at Schubert Theater (Australian tour group, improvisational and group tap to heavy rock music).

- Thoroughly read a newspaper you've never read.
- Go for an entire week without watching television.
- Attend a rally of a political persuasion different than your own.
- Do one of your employee's jobs for a shift.

The process of theoretical sampling helps a leader develop his own point of view. The leader must accept staff and analyst reports as just pieces of an overall concept. He can use it as a place to start but cannot rely on it as reality. The picture of reality may include political agendas or other frames of reference that can steer the unknowing leader in a direction that is not consciously chosen by the leader or developed in a dialogue with others. Therefore, the leader must develop listening, reading and observational skills to sample other points of view, develop his own theory and come to his own conclusions.

Notes:

(1) Hales, Colin. *What do Managers Do? A Critical Review of the Evidence*. Journal of Management Studies, 23:1, January, 1986.
(2) Glaser, Barney and Anselm Strauss. The Discovery of Grounded Theory: Strategies for Qualitative Research. Aldine, 1967, pg. 45.
(3) For more information on theoretical sampling see, Auerbach, Carl and Louise Silverstein. Qualitative Data. New York University Press, 2003.
(4) Lopez, Barry. Arctic Dreams: Imagination and Desire in a Northern Landscape. Bantam, 1987, pg. 101.
(5) Schein, Edgar. Organizational Culture and Leadership. Jossey-Bass, 1985, pg. 109.
(6) Benedict, Ruth. Patterns of Culture. Houghton Mifflin, 1934, pp. 1-2.

The Ramp Guy

The worth of great customer service requires a focus, not on the transactional costs, but on the relationship value.

Chip Bell

You can kiss the job Parking Attendant goodbye. You know, the drones that post your amount due and collect it without actually acknowledging your existence? They are being replaced by an automated system (with the same personality attributes as the drones) where you stick your parking ticket in a machine, its reads what you need to pay and then you place your credit card, voucher or real money into the machine and it gives you a paid receipt that you stick into the other end of the machine on your way out. It is simple, efficient and labor saving. However, there are a few bugs from time to time, not so much with the machines, but often with people who don't know how to use the system. They forget their ticket in their car, don't know how to place their debit card in the slot, or don't know how to place their voucher in front of the slot so it can be properly read. So, there does need to be an attendant to solve these problems, call service when it is needed and act as a security official.

At least that is what one might think.

Meet Juancho. He is the day attendant at the Eleventh Street & Harmon Place parking garage in downtown Minneapolis. I visit it weekly or more frequently as it is now where University of St.

Thomas faculty and students park, as well as people who work at Target and other firms in the vicinity. He does all the needed things required of the automated ticketing system detailed above. However, he has elevated what he does to the level of a parking garage concierge.

On a hot morning recently, he greeted me (as usual) at the ticketing machine. He was in his early morning position standing in the sunshine, hands joined behind his back, his tan, Harmon Place-labeled baseball cap in place, with the usual enthusiastic and friendly smile on his face. His full, black goatee was trimmed neatly. His look was completed by his tan, official ramp shirt, blue jeans and black, Adidas running shoes. He asked how late I would be. When I told him I would be there until about five p.m., he said, "It will be in the mid nineties by then," and suggested that I park in the basement so that my car would be cooler when I returned. On another day, he forewarned me there would be quite a lot of dignitaries attending the grand opening of the new School of Entrepreneurship later in the week taking up most of the ramp. He said that if I were to be on campus that day what to do to ensure that I had a place to park, even if it couldn't be in his ramp. Later in the day, he is often positioned between the elevators and ticketing machines showing people how to use the machines, asking if they have any questions or need to be walked to their cars for safety reasons. He also acts as an elevator use facilitator pressing the up and down buttons or holding the elevator doors open for business people and academics who have their hands occupied with cell phones and tickets. I recently overheard him remind a patron that the machine that was reading her UST voucher was a little slow in comparison to the machine next to it. He suggested that next time she use the other machine because it is more efficient. "It will save you a moment of your valuable time," I heard him say politely. Two weeks ago, he gave me a quarter out of his pocket to complete my transaction as I was fumbling with a handful of change, my briefcase and a cast on my right hand. He always says goodbye or good night in a warm and authentic way. He is very personable and friendly, yet professional.

I often tell a joke about the future of factory automation. In the future, the joke goes, a manufacturing plant will only have one employee and a dog. The person is there to feed the dog. The dog is there to bite the person if he attempts to touch any of the equipment. I now view this as a negative view of humanity as workers, as a result of my parking garage experience. I think I will add that another view is that a person needs to be there to be a good will ambassador for the plant, a solver of problems and an initiator of activities to add value to the customer experience.

Automating menial tasks frees the person up for other more value added activities.

Lessons Learned:

1. Automation is not only about labor savings, it can provide the opportunity for higher value work to take its place.
2. Any job can be reinvented and enlarged by a person with vision, energy and great human relations skills.

3. Parking costs the same on Eleventh & Harmon as elsewhere but the experience is far more valuable than any other car park I know.
4. The next time you are in downtown Minneapolis, give it a try!

5.5. Focus on the Whole and on the Interrelationships.

Anthropological work is holistic and integrative. It is holistic in that the researcher must look at what he is studying in its entirety. By integrative is meant that one must pay close attention to the *systemness* of what he is attempting to understand; how it works together. The concept of systems has been around since the 1940's when Ludwig von Bertalanffy's studies of phenomena that existed across scientific disciplines were published (1). He and others created General Systems Theory which looked into the interdependencies in social systems The physicist Fritjof Capra, summarizing this body of work, states that the first and most fundamental principle of systems theory is that systems are integrated wholes whose properties cannot be reduced to those of smaller parts. Their essential or "systemic" properties are properties of the whole, which none of their parts has (2). Capra suggests further that a key feature of systems thinking is the ability to shift one's attention back and forth from the parts and the whole; between system levels.

The concept of systems has become a central theme in the social sciences and is used significantly by physical and social sciences (3) and is a key philosophical construct by anthropologists who view the world as cultural ecologies (4). Draper Kauffman, for example, defines a system as, "A collection of parts which interact with each other to function as a whole. (5)" The basics of systems theory have made their way into the business literature as well. Jamshid Gharajedaghi's Managing Chaos and Complexity (6), for example, combines modern theory from the new complexity science with key elements of systems theory as described above. He states:

While the organization as a whole is becoming more and more interdependent, its parts increasingly display choice and behave independently. The resolution of this dilemma requires a dual shift of paradigm. The first shift will result in an ability to see the organization as a multiminded, sociocultural system, a voluntary association of purposeful members who have come together to serve themselves by serving the needs of the environment... The second shift will help us see through chaos and complexity and learn how to deal with an interdependent set of variables (6, pg. 9).

The analysis of a system reveals its fundamental structure and how it works. It provides the insight required to make it work more effectively and to repair it when it is not functioning properly. Understanding systems also helps one to gauge their nature, purpose and capacity for change. Recognizing a system's self-healing and self-managing properties also helps to know when to leave it alone.

To see and understand systems, we must be conscious of our thinking and categorization processes. Systems thinking is quite different than analytical thinking, the kind of thinking we generally learn in school. Russ Ackoff (7), one of the most prolific and interesting writers on systems theory, compares analytical and systems thinking, which he refers to as synthesis thinking.

1. In analysis, something that we want to understand is first taken apart. In synthesis, that which we want to understand is first identified as a part of one or more larger systems.
2. In the second step of analysis, an effort is made to understand the behavior of each part of a system taken separately. In the second step of synthesis, an effort is made to understand the function of the larger system(s) of which the whole is a part.
3. In analysis, the understanding of the parts of the system to be understood is then aggregated in an effort to explain the behavior or properties of the whole. In synthesis, the understanding of the larger containing system is then disaggregated to identify the role or function of the system to be understood (7, pp. 11 - 13).

There are many ways to learn principle five. The simplest way to focus on the whole and interrelatedness of a system is simply to pay closer attention to the most important elements of a particular business situation or process. For example, watch people working on the production of a product, whether it is in a manufacturing setting or in an office. What are the important parts of the cultural situation? Begin by taking an inventory of everything that is there from a systems point of view. Your list will start with the physical environment including the space and equipment and how they are laid out. Another part of the system will be the larger building of which this area is a part. A third part will include the overall purpose, structure and performance of the business in its competitive environment. Finally, include the people that are working on the product. What are their ages, genders, ethnicities, etc.? Are they working together, alone or in some parallel fashion? What is their disposition or orientation to their work? Look for patterns and relationships between the various parts in addition to simply cataloging the various elements. Sketching a diagram to show the key elements and their relationships is a more advanced step as it causes you to put pencil to paper and check your thoughts over time. Look at the diagram tomorrow and the next day. Does it still seem right? If you gain a new insight as you tinker with it that is all right. Draw a new diagram. But, don't throw the old one away. Number your diagrams so that you can review the progression of your thought process.

Don't get overwhelmed by the complexity of the situation you are observing. You didn't go from crawling one day to skipping rope the next. Over time your diagrams and observations will become more purposeful, easier to complete and more fruitful.

A second way to learn principle five is to describe the culture you are studying via a more complete template (8). *The Cultural Dynamics Model* (see Table 5.5.1. Cultural Dynamics Model, page 181) is based on work I have done over the years both in my academic and business life. I have used the model with MBA students in various classes as an assignment to help them learn about corporate culture and to develop their perspective. The topics they have chosen include business topics like *The Human*

"One of the most damaging misconceptions plaguing most people, including managers, is that problems are objects of direct experience. Not so: they are abstractions extracted from experience by analysis. Problems are related to experience as atoms to tables. Tables are experienced, not atoms. We are never confronted with separable problems but with situations that consist of complex systems of strongly interacting problems. I call such systems of problems *messes*. Therefore, the behavior of a mess depends more on how its parts interact than how they act independently of each other... Most people, including managers, do not generally know how to deal effectively with messes, with reality taken as a whole (7, pg. 13)."

Russ Ackoff

Implications of Implementing a New Information Technology System to *The Culture of Safety in a Small Commuter Airline* to *Trying to Understand the Culture of the New Company I Just Joined.* Or they focus on social settings including *The Coffee Shop, the Summer Family Softball Tournament, A Night in a Homeless Shelter and The Health Club Culture.* Over the course of several weeks they observe, ask questions and practice the principles outlined in this guide. They are armed with new lenses and skills.

Getting Started

Choose a business or social setting to study to develop a larger systems perspective. To use the model, begin by jotting down ideas for each of the categories. As you develop more information, add it to the template to enhance your understanding. Draw pictures and take photographs if it helps. Look for dynamics between the parts of the cultural system. Remember that you are attempting to understand a complex and dynamic system so look at the relationships between the components of the cultural system. When you get to the point where you feel you have some deeper level of understanding, you have developed a more systemic view of the whole and the interrelationships.

An advanced step in the cultural description and analysis process is to pay closer attention to a specific dilemma the organization or an individual is facing. For example, if leaders are facing a competitive challenge from a new entrant to their industry, how do they respond? Do they reflect on their historical assumptions and cultural ways, or do they attempt to find assistance from outside of their culture? Or, if an organization is building a new corporate headquarters building, how should the design of the new physical space be conceptualized in cultural terms? What historical artifacts and cultural symbols should be transferred to the new space? Which shouldn't be? Do new symbols need to be created? Why or why not?

A Case Study

A fictionalized company provides an interesting example to show the dynamics of *The Whole and the Interrelationships*. I will describe their culture and a dilemma they faced using the *Cultural Dynamics Model.*

1. Historical Cultural Assumptions. AMC started as a small engineering firm. Three young guys who attended college together, who had their first jobs in big and impersonal engineering firms, decided to start their own firm in 1997. In 2006, it had grown to thirteen people providing mainly job shop activities to larger engineering companies and had reached annual revenues of $1.1 million. Their culture was driven by truly blue collar values. The founders grew up in big families in rural towns in the Midwest and went to college at a small state university. They worked their way through college but did have some help financially from their parents. Their idea of fun was fishing, playing golf on public courses and getting the total organization and families together several times a year for a backyard

barbeque. Their organization was a blend of strong interpersonal ties, warm relationships and very little delineation of titles, jobs or responsibility. Informality, they thought, was a key to running a personable, family oriented, customer sensitive business. They were earning a good living and enjoying their growth as a company but were seeing storm clouds on the horizon.

2. Setting. AMC has a five year lease on the manufacturing center where their work is done. It is in a small town thirty miles west of a major Midwestern city. As opposed to more strategic marketing activities, most of their work is with the companies that they used to work for and other clients they have built through relationships. All of their clients are within an eighty mile radius of their headquarters. Their manufacturing center, which they call their *shop*, is comprised of a number of machines used to cut, shape and assemble simple sheet metal parts that are used to house motors and gears of machines produced by other manufacturers.

3. Assumptions. As stated in the earlier references to culture, assumptions are developed as leaders solve problems, develop solution mechanisms, use and perfect those solution processes over time and socialize other employees into the assumptions and processes around them. AMC developed internal organizational assumptions around the importance of family, informal relationships, high quality custom job shop work and personalized

customer relationships. These assumptions were solutions to issues the company faced early on. Stories are told over a beer at the local tavern about how these values were galvanized into the culture of the company. The stories accentuated the nature of financially important work, the way to find, treat and build customer relationships and the satisfaction that comes with producing reliable, quality products.

4. <u>Social Group Relationships</u>. The social groupings at AMC are based in the values and historical experiences of the founders. These include a minimum of formality and overlapping job responsibilities. The only real difference in the social structure of the company is that the founders are considered to be more important to the success of the company than hourly employees, even though the founder-owners downplay this at every opportunity. There is a respect for the founders given their success and the success and nature of the company's culture.

5. <u>Tasks</u>. The task structure at AMC is quite simple. There are a few, key customers that make up about 80% of AMC's business. Most of the machinery is set up to make parts for them. The production runs are high and consistent across their fiscal year. Twenty percent of their work varies from quarter to quarter based on a few companied who have small needs and a few new clients that they are trying to do more business with. So, AMC's historical

Table 5.5.1. Cultural Dynamics Model

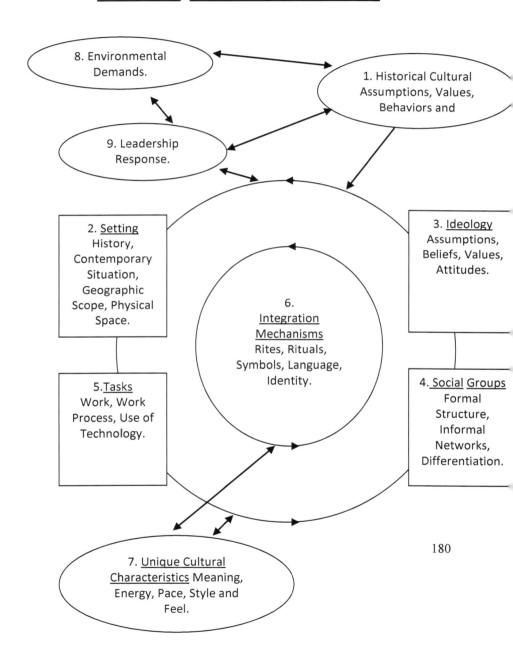

growth is based on the success and growth of their key customer group.

6. Integration Processes. The company is integrated in the values and experiences of the founder-owners. They frequently tell stories of their happiness and success moving from the bureaucratic big companies to a small, privately-held company that is highly personal and entrepreneurial. These values are also embedded in the family potluck and backyard barbeques, and the annual group fishing trips and the golf tournament. Trophies are awarded to employees who catch fish or not and the golf tournament banquet is replete with gifts for everyone. Notice how the events and rewards (rites and rituals) reinforce the values of the company marking its identity or personality as a firm.

7. Unique Cultural Characteristics. You can probably get a feel for the meaning, energy and pace of AMC based on reading the previous, descriptive paragraphs. The meaning is based in the historical experiences of the founders, early business successes and the strong, loyal and productive relationships with a few key companies that have created a stable and secure work experience for employees.

8. Environmental Demands. In 2008 their business barely made a profit. This was due to a sluggish manufacturing economy and the deep recession. AMC's key customers were not making money and were reducing their

inventories. In 2007, AMC's key customer initiated a supply chain initiative to reduce the number of suppliers, beat them down on cost and made decision making more objective and based less on personal histories. During this time some competitors were also consolidating with others through mergers and acquisitions. Less robust companies declared bankruptcy. The stronger, acquiring companies were attempting to broaden their skills, portfolios of products and services and shrink their infrastructure to lower cost and improve efficiency.

9. Leadership Response. AMC's initial leadership response to these new environmental demands was to go back to old, proven ways of operating. They worked their internal relationship-based culture and continued to work on enhancing their relationship with their key customers as well as infrequent customers and past customers. They told themselves that they had gotten away from their fundamentals and they needed to get back to them and work harder. 2009 was a better year for AMC financially, but to make their numbers they laid off three machine workers who had been with the company for five to seven years. The lay off caused a breach in the relationship-based culture and brought a great deal of uncertainty and anxiety to the company as a whole. That summer, during the owner's fishing trip, they decided that they needed to do something vastly different if they were going to survive as a company. As they discussed their challenges a new strategy emerged. They decided that they need to acquire

or merge with another engineering company. They would look for a company that could broaden their skill base and that would have different but complimentary products, services and a broader diversity of customers.

AMC found and completed a merger with KMO Enterprises in late 2009 becoming KAMCO ENTERPRISES. The combined company was thirty-one employees with a combined revenue of $2.9 million. It offered a broader spectrum of skills, products and services to their total set of customers. Shortly after the deal was worked out, there was a celebration for all employees and their families at the private golf club of one of the founders of KMO. Leading up to the celebration, there were many interesting conversations shared separately between former KMO senior employees and between senior AMC employees. The KMO people, through the negotiations, had found the AMC executives to be unorganized, too laid back in their approach to work and poorly educated. They made fun of AMC's small town feel, casual work attire, fishing trips and state college educations. The AMC executives on the other hand, talked about the elitist KMO executives, their Ivy League MBA's, lavish lifestyles and cookie cutter organizational structure. The celebration was characterized by AMC employees eating chips, sorting through the beer menu trying to find a brand they recognized and walking in small groups around the golf club's lavish grounds. The KMO employees sat on the deck or by the pool and drank martinis or beers from trendy craft brewers with upscale canapés supplied by the servers.

Without consciously knowing it at this point, KAMCO ENTERPRISES had successfully merged their businesses from a business point of view, but had created a whole new set of issues to deal with having to do with the huge cultural differences between the senior managers and the cultures of their respective organizations.

Journaling

A third way to develop the skill of *Seeing the Whole and the Interrelationships* is through journaling. Take notes after and before business experiences you have. Then, over time, reread your reflections to see if your ideas and observations have change or stayed the same and why. Another form of journaling is the art of story writing and telling about cultural experiences. I have experimented with writing stories about cultural experiences, which have helped my perspective. Through story telling, one can illustrate the limitations of the current perspective that is employed and show the learning points for reframing one's point of view. Try to be holistic and integrative in your story telling. Use one or a combination of the approaches offered above. Developing perspective or cultural wisdom, story telling and journaling go hand in hand. Our experience becomes our story if we can tell it. By telling our stories, we share our perspective so that others can learn from it. This is an important part of the art, the practice and the essence of leadership. Lastly, it is important to weave emotional elements into your work. They bring the drama of life into the cultural equation.

Being able to think about the whole and the interrelationships requires a systems point of view. One must attempt to picture or see systems and their dynamic interrelationships (9, 10). A system is a whole entity that is comprised of subsystems that are engaged in dynamic interrelationships. Utilizing a framework helps the aspiring systems thinker by providing some common elements of different types of system. The *Organizational Dynamics Model* provides a systems view of organizational culture. As you get familiar with its use, you may see parts of the system you are studying that this model does not cover. Take advantage of the learning opportunity and begin to create your own systems model.

Join your journey into seeing and modeling systems with note keeping and journaling. As you model, take notes about what you are studying, why you are studying it and any insights you have. Also take note of questions needing further investigation. Summarize your observations and thoughts on systems. Review your note before you begin your next research step. You are developing the skill of Understanding the Whole and the Interrelationships.

Notes:

(1) Bertalanffy, Ludwig von. "Der Organismus als Physikalisches System Betrachtet." *Die Naturwissenschaften*, vol. 28, pp. 521-531, 1940
(2) Capra, Fritjof. The Web of Life. Anchor, 1996, pp. 36-37.

(3) Bertalanffy, Ludwig von. General Systems Theory. Braziller, 1968.

(4) For an introduction to cultural ecology see, www.indiana.edu/~wanthro/eco.htm or Kerns, Virginia. Scenes from the High Desert: Julian Steward's Life and Theory. University of Illinois Press, 2003.

(5) Kaufman, Draper. Systems I. Future Systems, Inc., 1980.

(6) Gharajedaghi, Jamshid, Managing Chaos and Complexity: A Platform for Designing Business Architecture (Second Edition). Elsevier, 2006, page 9.

(7) Ackoff, Russell. Re-Creating the Corporation. Oxford University Press, 1999.

(8) Mirocha, John. *Corporate Culture: Methodology, Theoretical Approaches and Applications*. "Futurics." Vol.5, No. 3, pp. 247-256, 1981.

(9) French, Wendell, Cecil Bell and Robert Zawacki. Organization Development and Transformation (Sixth Edition). McGraw-Hill, 2005, pp. 47-49.

(10) Oshry, Barry. Seeing Systems: Unlocking the Mysteries of Organizational Life. Berrett-Koehler, 2007.

What it Takes to Build a Culture with a Strong Sense of Community

Isn't every part of life an experiment?

Neil M. (Princeton freshman)

I've learned quite a bit about culture and community in the past few weeks. I haven't done this by reading the business management literature or by attending a guru's workshop. My learning has come from attending a number of high school graduation parties.

The parties began the weekend before the actual graduation ceremony and continued for two and one half weeks after the actual graduation ceremony. They occurred on weekends and on weekday evenings. Some featured inexpensive fare and others shrimp and cold cut platters catered by the local deli. Some were held in the garage while others were held in the back yard. The weather was sunny for some and rainy for others. Across all of these differences, a few key elements of worth to business leaders were observable.

1. Preparation is key. Each of the celebrating parents had worked long and diligently to get their homes ready for the event. They planned, painted, weeded, cleaned, organized and cooked. On first impression, one might think that the parents and their families did this to *put their best foot first* or to show off their home or gardens.

However, upon looking closer, one could see that the purpose of the cleaning and cooking and other preparation was to provide a comfortable and enjoyable environment for the guests. It wasn't about pretense. It was about caring.

2. <u>More is better</u>. At Kelly's party (Taylor University), I noticed that a number of the attendees had lists of the parties they were attending. The list included the graduate's name, address and the time of the party. Some of the lists also ordered the names in the sequence they would be attended in. I guess that maps were even used to plot the most efficient order given the location of the parties. The really advanced lists, like Dan's (University of Puget Sound) had projected times to stay at each party and commute times between the homes. When you must attend thirteen parties in one afternoon you need to have a plan. The celebration attendees saw each other often during the two and one half week span of events. Every person was not invited to every party or the same parties. But, when invited to a celebration, they made their best effort to get to every party they were invited to. Women and women and women and men greeted one another most often with hugs. Guys greeted guys with the usual high fives or, "Hey." The connecting and reconnecting process never seemed to get old. In fact, it seemed to increasingly be emotional and strengthen the bonds between the individuals.

3. <u>The celebrations were real</u>. I have attended hundreds, maybe even thousands of celebrations in my life. I have been to births, weddings, team parties, keggers, proprovinas (the Polish celebration the day after a funeral), to name a few. Many of these celebrations were hollow to me. They lacked a clear connecting point between and among the attendees. They lacked a sense of excitement, joy and purpose that are so important to a true celebration. The graduation parties, in comparison, all had these critical elements. They all seemed to have taken root for the graduates in their prior relationships in the neighborhood, during the Honors Physics group project, in the band room, on the study trip abroad, on the court or the field and at Perkins after the big game. In other words, these graduation celebrations were not events that were isolated from other isolated events over time. The graduation celebrations were another, special, connecting point in a long and rich history of the graduates' excited, joyful, energized and purposeful lives. The parties were special because they truly marked a transition point between what was and what is to be for the graduates and their families. Maybe it is just because of the power of the teenage years. But, I doubt it. There is a real energy that you can actually feel that is genuine rather than contrived. It isn't a special event unrelated to other processes and events planned and orchestrated by meeting planners and management consultants. This stuff comes from the heart as well as the mind and it builds over time.

4. It was about the graduates. No egos were present in the givers of the parties. The parents and grandparents were in the background as servers, welcomers, and supporters. While both the parents and the graduates worked hard to earn the right for the child to graduate, the parties were about the graduates. In fact, each home had what we began calling a "shrine room" to the graduate. The room contained childhood pictures, family pictures, pictures of friends and various awards won by the graduate. One room even contained the crutches and air cast worn by a wounded basketball player during her season. Molly's (St. Cloud State University) shrine filled the walls of her parent's two-stall attached garage. They had a video of her pictures sequenced to some of her favorite music.

5. Stories, Stories, Stories. Stories were shared, laughs were laughed and memories were established and deepened, unifying the individuals even further. At Erin's party (Lafayette College), for example, the boys were throwing log after log on the bonfire in the woods. Being a little concerned, I asked Joe (Iowa State University) to be in charge of the fire and to limit how big it got. All of a sudden, several of the guys started to laugh. Then a few said sarcastically, "I'm not sure Joe is the best choice." Then they told me a story. Evidently, after school was out, many of the guys had a bonfire to celebrate the end of school. They symbolically burned their class notes to mark the end of the era. But, Joe went a little further. He burned all of his clothes and participated in the rest of the

festivities in his boxers. This situation kicked off a flurry of tellings of the Joe story as party goers mingled throughout the evening. My guess is that this story, as well as many of the others I heard, will be told for many years to come, continuing the graduation and life transition celebration... and preparation for what lies ahead.

Lessons Learned:

1. A great source of knowledge and insight can be derived from understanding the simple events around us.
2. Cultures with a strong sense of community are important to us as we face the critical transitions in our lives.
3. There is no quick, simple, magical recipe for developing a fist (a strong and united team). It takes shared experiences, building on successes and failures, time, patience and genuine, old-fashioned hard work and caring.

6. *Metacognition: Focus, Personal Discipline and the Five Insights.*

So, what have we learned as we have taken this journey together? Hopefully you now have a glimpse into the mind of an anthropologist who works in business. Hopefully, you have also learned about and practiced some of the skills that the Five Insights exercises have taught.

The next step is to develop a disciplined process of refreshing and deepening your thinking and perspective with the aid of the Five Insights. I call this process metacognition. The short definition of metacognition is "thinking about thinking (1)." Metacognition is the understanding and awareness of one's own mental or cognitive processes. It is an important concept in both psychology and educational psychology (2, 3). As you become more aware of and understand your thinking process better, you can identify its elements and systematic relationships. You can also introduce new factors and modify the systematic relationship dynamics to improve the functioning of your thought process.

Five Insights Diagnostic Survey

Completing the *Five Insights Diagnostic Survey* is a first step in this process (see next page). Circle your answers to the five questions in the survey on the next page. Note that there are two parts to each question, (a) an assessment of your current skill level and (b) an assessment of your developmental needs. Once you have completed the survey take note of the areas that

Five Insights Diagnostic Survey

This diagnostic survey is designed to help you assess your current skills on the Five Insights and to point to areas needing strengthening. Rate yourself on the following items (a) and then assess your developmental needs (b). Use 1 as low and 5 as high.

1. Look beneath the surface.
    a. My current skills.
        1   2   3   4   5
    b. My developmental needs.
        1   2   3   4   5

2. You Are a Part of the System You Are Participating In.
    a. My current skills.
        1   2   3   4   5
    b. My developmental needs.
        1   2   3   4   5

3. Participant Observation.
    a. My current skills.
        1   2   3   4   5
    b. My developmental needs.
        1   2   3   4   5

4. Theoretical Sampling.
    a. My current skills.
        1   2   3   4   5
    b. My developmental needs.
        1   2   3   4   5

5. Focus on the Whole and on the Interrelationships.
    a. My current skills.
        1   2   3   4   5
    b. My developmental needs.
        1   2   3   4   5

you scored high on (4's and 5's) and the areas you scored low on (1's and 2's) for the *current skill level*. What is your highest score and lowest score? Now do the same for your *developmental needs*. What is your highest score and lowest score? Lastly, compare your scores for *current skill level* with those for *developmental needs*. Note any significant gaps between high scores for *developmental needs* and moderate or low scores on *current skill level*. If you have a gap between a *developmental need* and a *current skill level*, ask yourself what you have to gain from developing the skill to be more like the score for the need. Then ask yourself what activities you will need to undertake to improve the score. Review the materials associated with that Insight in the previous parts of this text.

1. My *current* skills:
2. High Scores _____
a. Low Scores _____

3. My *developmental* needs:
a. High Scores _____
b. Low Scores _____

4. Comparison and Gap Analysis: Low *current* skills with high *developmental* needs.

5. Activities needed to raise the *current* skills to meet the *developmental* needs

This exercise helps you identify your strengths and developmental needs using the Five Insights of perspective. It also helps you develop an individual development plan for strengthening the insight discipline. Work the activities for three months and then reassess yourself to see if you have changed.

Patterns and Sequences

The next step is to identify the sequence in which you currently use the five insights. When I started working with the Five Insights, I ordered the sequence of subchapters the way I thought was the most beneficial. To test my idea, I have asked students to rank order the top three Insights in the order that they currently use them and then to rank order the top three in the order that they think they should use them to improve their leadership perspective. Then I had small groups of students discuss their current and needed priorities. Finally, I had the small groups identify the top three that they believed were most important overall for developing leadership perspective. Needless to say the results were eye opening.

There were individuals who said that they have an over-pronounced need to stay at the big picture level. Others wanted to practice participant observation but recognized that they were uncomfortable relating to people in some ways. Finally, most agreed that a truly developed perspective means that one can use the Five Insights as needed in situations that require different cognitive processes. Here are three examples.

Molly. A nurse by training and profession, Molly is used to working with data, regulation, strict processes and facts. Patients, she says, are almost an afterthought. Her concern as she moves into nurse management is being able to see the forest without losing sight of the trees. She still needs to be on top of the processes and facts but now she will be more concerned with ensuring the proper oversight of those processes and the nurses that collect and process them. Her perspective, she says, has been very focused on details and less on oversight and the management of people. Her current listing of her top three Insights are as follows:

1. Look Beneath the Surface.
2. You are a part of the Cultural System You are Participating In.
3. Theoretical Sampling.

She *Looks Beneath the Surface* to try to be more sure of what is really going on with the data she collects so she is sure of her accuracy. She realizes that she is *Part of the System* and that accountability is very important in her work: no one to blame but herself. A distant third Insight is *Theoretical Sampling*. She says that she uses the process to build theories of why mistakes are made or numbers don't add up.

Moving to management will require a different emphasis and order. Her developmental priorities are:

1. Focus on the Whole and Interrelationships.

2. Participant Observation.
3. Theoretical Sampling.

The *Whole and Interrelationship* is her forest. She needs a bigger picture thought process to have a perspective on activities and issues as she manages her shift nurses. *Participant Observation for* her is management by walking around: observing, participating in and observing nurse, nurse-doctor, nurse-nurse, and nurse-patient activities and conducting informal interviews with staff and patients to make sure her view is fresh and relatively unfiltered. She has constructed a template to use to guide her shift activities to ensure that she uses the developmental sequence rather than relying on her natural pattern. The natural pattern served her well as a technician but could be problematic if over utilized as she is now a manager.

Tomas. Tomas is the Director of Information Services for his publicly traded manufacturing firm. The firm has decided to implement an ERP (Enterprise-wide Resource Planning) system to help optimize and integrate internal and external management information across his entire organization, embracing finance/accounting, manufacturing, sales and service, customer relationship management. He is partnering with an external IT firm to get the job done. To ensure integration between his staff and the consultants, he has created an ERP Steering Committee to coordinate activities. He is the Chairperson.
Overseeing the execution of the ERP system in addition to Tomas' management of every day activities will stretch the scope, complexity and uncertainty of his job given the headaches that

come with systems conversion projects. His top three Insights are as follows:

1. Focus on the Whole and the Interrelationships.
2. Look Beneath the Surface.
3. Theoretical Sampling.

He uses *The Whole and the Interrelationships* to provide a wide lens to oversee the activities of his large department. He also needs to concentrate on the interdependencies between corporate IT and the IT departments in the seven business units of his firm. There are common goals and business processes. He *Looks Beneath the Surface* to drill down into problems and help his managers trouble shoot issues. He says through this practice he develops really good questions to ask during staff meetings and one-on-ones with his managers. He *Theoretically Samples* broader aspects of the business including finance, manufacturing and customer service during his senior staff meetings to develop a broader appreciation for how the whole business operates.

As Tomas looks at his new role as the chairperson of the Steering Committee he sees a slightly different pattern.

1. You are a Part of the Cultural System You Are Participating In.
2. Focus on the Whole and the Interrelationships.
3. Participant Observation.

He has realized that he has definite ideas about the ERP implementation project. He knows that he is a *Part of the Cultural System he is Participating In* and that he needs to be aware of his espoused theories and his theories in use. Any conflict between the two could cause serious issues with implementation and team cohesion. He must remain focused on the Whole and the Interrelationships as piecemeal implementation will cause overall system integration issues. Finally he knows he has a lot to learn on the move. His ideas will certainly change over time. He needs to observe and work with the contractors as well as his staff and the Steering Committee not always as an authority but as a partner in the learning and change process.

Rich. Rich is the President and CEO of a medium-sized company in the industrial air filtration business. Growth has been very difficult in the U.S. because of over capacity in the industry and very strong competition. Rich's board of directors recently gave approval for the company's first acquisition outside of North America. They acquired a small, family-held firm in Poland. The acquisition was a great idea on paper. The plant was located ideally to serve growth markets in Eastern Europe and also to sell into Western Europe because of Poland's low wage rates. The financials looking ahead were very strong. Rich is about to make his first trip to the company and plant since the acquisition last quarter. Profits are a fraction of what the projections were and product quality is not what it needs to be. Rich is cognizant that he might need to look at the situation in Poland with "a fresh set of eyes." His current top three Insights are:

1. Theoretical Sampling.
2. Focus on the Whole and the Interrelationships.
3. Look Beneath the Surface.

Rich's background before becoming the President and CEO of this firm was in management consulting. He worked for a strategy firm and specialized in international growth. That is why the board offered him this job two years ago. He had been successful by strategically viewing industries for emerging opportunities as he *Theoretically Sampled* the prospectuses of various companies and thought of emerging opportunities for them. He needed to ground his thinking in the strategy of the firm he was working with so he needed to think about potential acquisition targets in terms of how they would fit with *The Whole and the Interrelationships*. Finally, Rich attempted to *Look Beneath the Surface* possibilities to see if the target was for real and would produce the intended results.

As Rich looks ahead to his visit to Poland he has an agenda that is supported by a different sequence of Insights.

1. You are a part of the Cultural System You are Participating In.
2. Focus on the Whole and the Interrelationships.
3. Participant Observation.

Rich has read about and experienced the post acquisition issues in acquired firms. He knows that projections can be inflated, that there could be cultural compatibility issues between his firm and the acquired firm and that there could be post acquisition motivation and productivity issues. As the President and CEO he knows that he is a *Part of the Cultural System he will be Participating In*. He needs to be aware of his possible impact on the group and will need to put the senior management team there at ease so that he gets quality information. He will need to keep his eye on *The Whole and the Interrelationships* both at the acquired company and as it relates to his international growth strategy. Lastly, he needs to be an astute *Observer* and use every opportunity to learn about the company on its own terms.

Each of these examples illustrates a situation where a person was being challenged by emergent leadership issues. Moving from technician to manager, adding steering committee responsibilities to those of a director and making a first international acquisition all require the person to stretch his or her skills beyond their current level of experience and skill. Each of these individuals had the wherewithal to know that they needed to get to the balcony and to shift their thinking to lead. Once the recognition of the need and the intention to lead are present a person is ready to act. Having a developmental framework in place can assist the emerging leader or the leader needing renewal to act with discipline. Remember that mastery means committing oneself to the journey. The journey will be long and the leader should savor it for its own meaning and significance and not savor only the eventual arrival at the destination.

Notes:

(1) http://www.kaplaneduneering.com/kappnotes/index.php/2010/08/definition-metacognition/
(2) Dunlosky, John and Janet Metcalfe. Metacognition. Sage, 2009
(3) Perfect, Timothy and Bennett Schwartz (Editors). Applied Metacognition. University of Cambridge, 2002.

Roadmap

Trust the process.

The change leader's refrain.

Amanda, a student in my Organization Development (OD) & Change Management class this summer, asked me a really interesting question that got me thinking. "John, Why is it that most OD projects fail?" After a few seconds of several different answers cycling through my mind, it was clear to me that the word *process* was central to all other examples. *"Process,"* I said, as I turned to write the word on the board, "is one of the most under-appreciated terms in change management."

I turned to see Amanda's eyes catch mine and I anticipated her follow up question, "Why?" Many managers, I responded (as she nodded in agreement to my accurately anticipating her question), think of process as a short, linear route between where they are and where they want to be, regardless of the scale and complexity of the task. Leaders, on the other hand, know that in more complex and uncertain circumstances, the route is more of a journey than a few, simple steps ahead. Managers get to where they are because they get things done, on time and on budget. They learn to work within the current business system or model that is full of orderly, quantifiable problems to solve that reap benefits for their companies. Their life is full of objectives, budgets, gant charts, process flows, from-to charts and value chains.

But then reality throws them a curveball. It presents a dilemma that isn't quite like the ones that they have become accustomed to solving and checking off on their to-do sheet for the day or week. The boundaries of the problem are unknown or unclear, the target may be blurry or appear differently to various stakeholders and the length of the journey and route are open to some speculation even though a timeline and a budget need to be prepared. And, the consequences aren't a simple employee lawsuit, a product rejection by a customer or minor inefficiencies. The stakes are more strategic and the consequences of failure or success are critical to the survival of the enterprise.

The term *roadmap* is contemporary jargon for a plan. That works when the problem fits the simple, rational, quantifiable, been-there-done-that model. However, roadmap doesn't apply when you get the curve ball, the slider or the change-up. Then it is more fitting to call it what it is: an exploration, an adventure or a journey. Calling the quasi-plan a roadmap sets the planners and implementers up for problems. It makes the challenge seem simpler and more straight forward than it really is. And secondly, it falsely allows leaders to form an expectation that it will be delivered on time and on budget and that nothing unusual will happen.

In complex and uncertain times, we should put the simple process models away and think more along the lines of Sir Ernest Shackleton's epic exploration of the Antarctic, Lewis and Clark's journey into the American Northwest or Frodo's journey in The

<u>Fellowship of the Ring</u> . When you plan an exploration or journey, process refers to how much planning, involvement and participation their needs to be given the perils, both known and unknown. This is where the leader really needs to think it through with trusted colleagues (kitchen cabinet). A set of additional taskforces, committees, design teams and other change management structures often need to be set in place, and boundaries, responsibilities and accountabilities must be clarified and coordinated. One also needs to install feedback milestones to check the actual versus the plan and work on contingencies or deal with new developments that could put the original plan in the shredder. This is where the leader must confront his process demons.

The process demons I have observed fall into the following categories.

1. ***Process Intolerence***. Many would-be leaders suffer from this malaise. By force of personality and/or as a result of living in an engineered work world, many individuals have difficulty tolerating facts that don't add up, long conversations to define and resolve messy issues that don't seem to go anywhere or lots of people involvement. They crave the solace of their PC, their cube or office and an Excel Spreadsheet or budget. These folks need to be pushed gently into challenges where they can't do it all by themselves and need to interact with others to make change happen. They need coaching from their supervisor or an external coach in the art and practice of charting a

course where they are not completely in control and must learn from the experience. They also need to develop a kitchen cabinet and learn to use other change management structures appropriately.

2. ***Haphazard Process***. A haphazard process is generally spawned by change management novices, employees who are new to a company and don't know how it works, employees who overuse committees and taskforces or individuals who have a hard time making decisions, sticking to them and staying the course. They allow individuals with the loudest voices, the last person they talked to, the committee or fear to make their decisions. They miss important deadlines, re-open questions that have been put to bed long ago, don't understand what is going on with the business and don't include in their thinking emerging ideas and facts that could cause a necessary change to be considered. They are adrift in the sea of change and process. As a consultant friend recently said when describing a change project she was working on, "This is an example of process run amok with rampant professional, business and project management incompetence!" These individuals should not be put in charge of large scale changes. They need to learn the basics of change leadership first as a follower and then under the tutelage of a more experienced leader or consultant in less controlled situations.

3. ***Overly Controlled Process***. Part of setting your mentality on adventure rather than a three step process is formed in the realization and anticipation that surprises will happen. Some individuals, fearing this will happen, grab the process by the horns and try to control something that cannot be controlled. Others merely apply simple roadmap ideas to a messy situation without even being aware that the simple roadmap is the wrong tool to use. An early coaching assignment of mine getting an experienced manager ready for a challenging assignment at a troubled plant ended with the manager shaking my hand and saying, "I'm gonna grab the business by the !@*#s and squeeze until it drops to its knees. Then I'll let up a little but never let go." The plant was shut down due to continued union issues and emerging industry changes less than a year later and Harold was retired. A significant shift of mind from the illusion of total control to a plan that is created with a *go with some flow* view is needed. Again, strong supervisory coaching can help this type of leader let go of the needs for complete control by showing the person the strength of his team and supporting him as he lets go with enabling structures and processes, such as a union management relations committee and a strategic planning process team in Harold's case. Of course, for the Harolds of the world, committees would be touchy feely crap!

Consultants need to be aware of these issues as well. Many consultants, not just managers, have their process demons. I, for example, can keep things too conceptual and discussion oriented for some of my process intolerant clients. I can't give in to their intolerance. But I can compromise a little and coach them through their discomfort with process. I have also over-controlled processes sometimes in areas where I have deep experience. I could let the client explore the terrain more but not so much that they do not benefit from my experience guiding them.

So, what are we to do with process? First, we must recognize our demons and settle them with a more rational and disciplined view of change. Second, we must recognize the demons of the client whether we are leaders or consultants. We cannot give into their issues, but we can challenge, teach and counsel them. Finally, the size, complexity and uncertainty of the change should guide how much process we need. The bigger the scope, the more uncertainty and the more complexity means more process—more involvement of people, less control of means and ends, committee structures to involved employees and a different role for the leader of change. In these situtaions, the change leader is more of a sponsor, facilitator, key influencer and strategist. He creates forums for discussion, identifies action teams to explore alternatives and coordinates the decision making. This doen't mean that he is off the hook in terms of responsibility and accountability. It just means that he can't do it all alone and needs to trust and work with and learn from his people and process.

Lessons Learned:

1. A roadmap isn't always characterized by a perfectly structured itinerary.

2. The term *roadmap* is overused today and can be misleading.
3. Big change needs to be framed with terms like exploration, adventure and journey to set the tone.
4. *Process* is a change leadership term that deserves respect, study and innovation.

7. *Conclusions*

Life runs, leaping and bounding out in front of us. If only we could view the future from its vantage point rather than ours as we hurry to keep up. Many of us are overwhelmed by the speed, complexity, competitiveness and ambiguity of this dynamic. We crave perspective.

Perspective is not about keeping up. It is about finding and staying on the forefront, even daring to create it. To do that, we must practice the Five Insights of <u>Perspective</u>: continuously looking beneath the surface, seeing yourself as a part of the culture you participate in, practicing participant observation, theoretically sampling views different than your own or of the mainstream, and focusing on the whole and on the interrelationships of our complex life and business situations. Seeking perspective requires an outward life of inquiry where action is tempered by understanding and sensitivity to the culture we find ourselves in. Maintaining and developing perspective necessitates reflection and experimentation with our own thought, logic and intentions to lead. In order to fully develop perspective (mastery) remember that the journey takes thousands of hours of inquiry, reflection and experimentation in the leader lab we call life and business. Have the curiosity, take the risk and develop the discipline to lead.

Here are a few questions to ask yourself to clarify your plan to develop your perspective. Ask yourself these questions frequently especially when you are being challenged by work which is beyond your experience and skill level. They will help you to develop as a leader.

1. I would describe my pre-**Perspective**, perspective as...

2. I would describe my current perspective as...

3. To improve my perspective I will...

4. If I take these steps to improve my perspective I will gain...

5. If I take these steps to improve my perspective my company will...

6. To improve our company's perspective we should...

Old Town Market

Toto, we are not in Kansas anymore!

Dorothy

Such a simple thing a bed is. Something I take for granted I realize. But not now, I muse, as my head hits the pillow at 4:30 a.m. in Hyderabad, India after 27 hours of travel to get there. I review what I have seen of India so far: a dilapidated airport out of a 1950's British film, dozens of people waiting for loved ones at 2:15 a.m. including married women in their brilliantly colored saris, beggars surrounding the bus and asking for money as we load and the long bumpy ride to the hotel traversing what seems to be countless construction sites, dark, sleepy parts of the city, squatter villages comprised of tents and makeshift structures of cardboard, cloth, wood and corrugated metal and truck traffic. Tomorrow (oops, later today) my real journey will start.

I awake at daylight and look out my hotel window. I see Microsoft and Infosys to the east, the Indian School of Business to the south and a large boulder laden ridge approximately a half mile wide running west to the horizon. Suddenly I hear a faint explosion and see a puff of smoke in the distance and realize that the ridge is actually a working, above ground rock quarry. I go back to bed to try to get a little more sleep.

After breakfast we hear a few *Welcome to India* speeches from our hosts. One of the presenters provides an overview of India and refers in some detail to the *Pyramid*. He talks about it is as a combination of Maslow's hierarchy of needs and the country's socio-economic distribution pattern. He mentions some statistics that paint the picture of India. India is at once an old, Asian civilization, and at the same time, a modern nation with democratic institutions with a population of 1.2 billion, lots of problems and lots of promise. It is the world's largest democracy with an incredibly diverse population including Hindus, Muslims (India has the third largest population in the world) Sikhs, Christians, Buddhists, Jains, Zoroastrians, Jews and animists. There are twenty-two official languages in India. The developing country is divided among a tiny affluent minority, a rising middle class and 800 million people who live on less than $2 per day. India faces all the critical problems of our time—extreme social inequality, employment insecurity, severe infrastructure problems including airports, water, electricity and roads, a growing energy crisis, a degraded environment, plus a galloping HIV/AIDS epidemic, and terrorist attacks—on a scale that defies the imagination. Reading about this is one thing...

My travel group gets on the bus after a simple, Indian buffet to explore the old town market of Hyderabad and experience firsthand, many of these startling facts. India uses the British traffic flow system where vehicles go in the opposite direction to what we Americans use. Well sort of. Where there are traffic signs, motorists seem to treat them as mere suggestions as vehicles of all types speed, swerve and compete for space and advancement opportunities regardless of what the signs state. At a few major intersections, there are traffic control officers wearing devices to filter the air (heavy with exhaust fumes and smoke) ranging from a simple scarf to a paper mask to a full blown industrial respiratory unit. The officers appear to be mostly obeyed as they hold up oncoming traffic by putting their palms out in a stop declaration allowing crossing traffic to proceed. While this is happening, motor bikes of all sizes drive between and around bigger vehicles to get to the front of the line. When the traffic control officer waves traffic on it is like he has waved a flag to start a motocross event! Vroom! On side streets anything and everything goes. An hour and fifteen minutes later we are in the center of the old city driving down a narrow, pothole filled street teeming with people and traffic. It appears chaotic. Trucks, motorized rickshaws, motorcycles with one to five people on them, vendors pushing large carts of produce, shoppers, cars, bicyclists, construction workers, hawkers and beggars are packed shoulder to shoulder and chest to back competing for space or attention or trying to get to where they are going. Everyone pushes, darts and works around each other trying to progress and not get run over by a vehicle.

It looks almost coordinated now as I study it. It is similar to the dance I have witnessed in Bangkok and San Paulo before but all of the elements seem to be magnified here. Trucks and autos rule in a pecking order of safety but are almost impossible to maneuver on the narrow roads and in heavy traffic. Small, fast, agile motorcycles and the three wheeled rickshaws make the most progress darting around bigger vehicles and through groups of people. Pedestrians and bicycle riders are at high risk and blend into the spaces between the larger vehicular competition. Those individuals pushing carts are careful and slow because of the low maneuverability of their carts, the uneven pavement and the precious nature of their cargo but the pushers can and do use their carts as a shield against aggressive motorcycle and rickshaw drivers. Beggars and hawkers follow their targets as if oblivious to the crowds and vehicles. Lost in trying to comprehend the street scene, I suddenly notice our bus is parking on the edge of the road in front of a business that services car radiators beneath a power line that looks like a gigantic hairball. Obviously local businesses have illegally tapped into the city's electrical system.

Getting off the bus and into the crowd is a surreal experience. We are now a part of the chaos and feel the 98 degree heat, struggle with the exhaust fumes from the trucks, cars, motorcycles and rickshaws (has anyone heard of a catalytic converter?) and are overwhelmed by the incessant honking as drivers jockey for position. We also experience the filth of the street that is comprised of construction debris, garbage and litter and the dust that is stirred up with all the movement on the antiquated street. Someone notices a man urinating against a building and directs our attention to it. Then we encounter a small group of goats being herded along by a shepherd. Add in a few dogs, cats and chickens and the Hyderabad Market scene gets more complete. The full experience is overwhelming to some of the group, a few of whom look surprised, appalled and fearful. Our guide Sudir states, "Keep moving in this direction please," just as he is hit and knocked down by a car trying to cut between two rickshaws and a group of construction workers. We rush to his aid. After a few seconds, he pops up and brushes himself off. He and the car

215

driver look at each other in a detached kind of way. He resumes his role as our leader hurrying us toward the epicenter of the market as the car continues its journey in the opposite direction. "No harm, no foul," a colleague states.

The market epicenter is teaming with thousands of people along a much larger road that runs north/south to the mostly east/west street we parked on. Stalls are set up along the road wherever there is room creating a small village of stalls selling everything from produce and flowers to furniture, toys, food, jewelry and textiles. (We learn from our guide that this part of the city is a self-regulating micro-economy with most goods and services being produced and consumed within a relatively small area. Only produce, fuel and a few dry goods are brought in and visitors buy and take locally made products out.) We swiftly and fearfully cross the street in twos and threes darting among and between the coordinated insanity that are Indian crowds and traffic.

We regroup near a flower market to catch our breath and try to find the Muslim Mosque, Mecca Masjid, built in 1617 by Muhammad Quili Qutb Shah, the fifth sultan of Hyderabad, which is our destination. The heat, air pollution, vehicular and people density and noise are almost unbearable. We notice that people are surrounding us looking at us like we are from another planet. Some reach out to touch us almost to see if we are real. I feel a young woman holding an infant scratch my pocket as beggars do there trying to get a few Rupees from me. The attention we are attracting is disconcerting and we must retrace our steps back across the street as we have gone in the wrong direction. Some members of our group are fearful so we break into groups with more seasoned travelers acting as traffic cops standing bravely in front of traffic to allow others to cross the road. Sudir points in a direction and yells to us to keep moving like he is driving a herd of cattle. We respond to his command.

A few minutes later, we arrive at the Mosque which is a reprieve from the chaos of the streets. It is in a no traffic zone that was created to prevent further deterioration of the buildings which have suffered greatly from the air pollution. We take off our shoes and entrust them to an ancient women who probably just assumed the role of Shoe Guard to collect Rupee tips for attending to our shoes. After our tour of the relics' area, said to contain a hair from the Islamic prophet Muhammad, we again draw a crowd of on-lookers as we put on our shoes and snap a few pictures. This time there are several children who approach us, shake our hands and practice their English speaking skills with us by asking our names. We comply eagerly and try to converse further, which is problematic. Then we are approached by a very old holy man who has been speaking to a crowd of people, I assume, about the history and significance of the Mosque and his beliefs. He too speaks a bit of English and asks us where we are from. When he hears a member of the party say, "America," he looks a bit dismayed but wags his head from side to side which, in India, means he understands but that he doesn't necessarily agree. We tell him that is time for us to go and we walk back into the market and to the bus. Given that it is now late afternoon, it takes two hours in the traffic, congestion and air and noise pollution to get back to the hotel.

<u>Lessons Learned</u>:

1. To truly learn about a place, one must see it in-person and experience it from the ground.
2. In a developing country, emphasize understanding the base of the pyramid first not the top or the middle.
3. You can't judge another culture from your experience. You have to assess it on its own terms.
4. Sometimes business travel is not for the faint of heart.

Namaste!

Appendix 1. NWA/Delta Timeline

- 1983-84 Merger with Republic Airlines
- 1980's-1990's International Business Growth
- 1980's-1990'sHidden Inefficiencies During Growth
- 2001, 911 Terrorist Attacks
- Attacks Reduce Airline Revenues
- Costs Soar and Revenues Decline Due to Security Issues and Decreased Passenger Activity
- 2000's Rise of Competitors
- Cost Cutting
- 2005 Bankruptcy and Re-structuring
- 2006 SARS and Bird Flu Reduce Travel to Asia
- Fleet Modernization and Route Consolidation
- 2007 Record Fuel Prices of $140 Per Barrel
- 2008 NWA /Delta Merger Proposed
- 2008 Recession
- 2008 Presidential Election
- 2008 Federal Economic Intervention
- 2009 NWA/Delta Merger Completed
- 2009 Flight Attendants Booed Announcing New Delta Apparel
- 2010 NWA and Delta Websites Merged
- 2011 Delta Pays $313 Million in Incentive Pay to Employees.
- 2011 Japan Earthquake, Tsunami and Nuclear Incident.
- 2011 Oil Approaches $100 Per Barrel
- 2011 Delta Cuts Services and 2,000 Jobs

Source: Minneapolis StarTribune

Notes

Ackoff, Russell. Re-Creating the Corporation. Oxford University Press, 1999, pp. 11-13.

Argyris, Chris and David Schon. Theory in Practice: Increasing Professional Effectiveness. Jossey-Bass, 1974.

Argyris, Chris and David Schon. Organizational Learning: A Theory of Action Perspective. Addison-Wesley, 1978.

Auerbach, Carl and Louise Silverstein. Qualitative Data. New York University Press, 2003.

Berg, Bruce. Qualitative Research Methods for the Social Sciences (Seventh Edition). Allyn and Bacon, 2005.

Benedict, Ruth. Patterns of Culture. Houghton Mifflin, 1934.

Bennett, John. Northern Plainsmen: Adaptive Strategy and Agrarian Life. Aldine,1969.

Bennis, Warren and R. Thomas. "Crucibles of Leadership." *Harvard Business Review*, 80 (9), 39, 2002.

Bernard, H. Russell and Gery Ryan. Analyzing Qualitative Data: Systematic Approaches. Sage, 2010.

Bertalanffy, Ludwig von. "Der Organismus als Physikalisches

System Betrachtet." *Die Naturwissenschaften*, vol. 28, pp. 521-531, 1940.

Bertalanffy,Ludwig von. General Systems Theory. Braziller, 1968.

Bolman, Lee and Terrance Deal. Reframing Organizations: Artistry, Choice, and Leadership (Fourth Edition). Jossey-Bass, 2008.

Bunker, Kerry, Douglas T. Hall and Kathy E. Kram (Editors). Extraordinary Leadership: Addressing the Gaps in Senior Executive Development. John Wiley & Sons, 2010.

Capra, Fritjof. The Web of Life. Anchor Books, 1996, pp. 36-37.

Chanda, Nayan. Bound Together: How Traders, Peachers, Adventurers, and Warriors Shaped Globalization. Yale University Press, 2007.

Charan, Ram, Stephen Drotter and James Noel. The Leadership Pipeline: How to Build the Leadership-Powered Company. Jossey-Bass, 2001.

Connor, Daryl. Managing at the Speed of Change. Villard, 1993.

Connors, Roger and Tom Smith. Change the Culture, Change the Game: The Breakthrough Strategy for Energizing Your Organization and Creating Accountability for Results. Portfolio, 2011.

Cowan, John. Small Decencies. HarperBusiness, 1992.

Cowan, John. The Common Table. HarperBusiness, 1995.

Cummins, H.J. "Generations Collide." *Minneapolis StarTribune*, Section D, pp 1-4, Sunday, November 27, 2005.

Deal, Terrance and Allan Kennedy. Corporate Cultures: The Rites and Rituals of Corporate Life, Addison-Wesley. 1982.

Deal, Terrance and Allan Kennedy. The New Corporate Cultures. Perseus, 1999.

De Geus, Arie. The Living Company. Harvard Business School Publishers, 2002.

Dunlosky, John and Janet Metcalfe. Metacognition. Sage, 2009

Fetterman, David. Ethnography: Step by Step, (Applied Methods). Sage, 2010.

Friedman, Thomas. The World is Flat: A Brief History of the Twenty-First Century. Farrar, Straus and Giroux, 2006.

Fick, Uwe. An Introduction to Qualitative Research. Sage, 2002.

French, Wendell, Cecil Bell and Robert Zawacki. Organization Development and Transformation (Sixth Edition). McGraw-Hill, 2005, pp. 47-49.

Geertz, Clifford. The Interpretation of Cultures. Basic Books, 1972.

Gharajedaghi, Jamshid. Systems Thinking: Managing Chaos and Complexity (Second Edition). Elsevier, 2006.

Heifitz, Ronald. Leadership Without Easy Answers. Harvard University Press, 1994.

Heifitz, Ronald and Marty Linsky. Leadership on the Line: Staying Alive through the Dangers of Leading. Harvard Business School Press, 2002.

Hoebel, E. Adamson. The Cheyennes: Indians of the Great Plains. Holt, Rinehart and Winston, 1960.

Kauffman, Draper. Systems I. Future Systems, Inc., 1980.

Kerns, Virginia. Scenes from the High Desert: Julian Steward's Life and Theory. University of Illinois Press, 2003.

Kirk, Jerome and Marc Miller. Reliability and Validity in Qualitative Research. Sage, 1986.

Kiste, Robert. The Bikinians: A Study in Forced Migration. Cummings, 1974.

Kotter, John. The Heart of Change. Harvard Business School Press, 2002, pp. 62-67.

Kluger, Jeffrey. Simplexity: Why Simple Things Become Complex (and How Complex Things Can Be Made Simple). Hyperion, 2008.

Locke, Karen. Grounded Theory in Management Research. Sage, 2001.

Lopez, Barry. Arctic Dreams: Imagination and Desire in a Northern Landscape. Bantam, 1987.

Madison, D. Soyini. Critical Ethnography. Sage, 2005.

McCall, Morgan W., Michael Lombardo and Ann Morrison. Lessons of Experience: How Successful Executives Develop on the Job. Lexington, 1988.

McCall, Morgan W. High Flyers: Developing the Next Generation of Leaders. Harvard Business School Press, 2002.

Mirocha, John. "Corporate Culture: Methodology, Theoretical Approaches and Applications." *Futurics*, Vol. 5, No. 3, Pergamon Press Ltd., 1981.

Morris , Michael, Kwo Leung, Daniel Ames and Brian Licke. "Views from Inside and Outside: Integrating Emic and Etic Insights about Culture and Justice Judgment." *Academy of Management Review*, 1999, Vol. 24. No. 1, 781-796.

Mouawad, Jad. "Sticking the Landing." *Minneapolis StarTribune*,

May 20, 2011, pg. D, 6.

Olson, Edwin and Glenda Eoyang. Facilitating Organizational Change. Jossey-Bass, 2001.

Oshry, Barry. Seeing Systems: Unlocking the Mysteries of Organizational Life. Berrett- Koehler, 2007.

Pascale, Richard, Mark Millemann and Linda Gioja. Surfing the Edge of Chaos. Three Rivers Press, 2000.

Pelto, Pertti. Anthropological Research: The Structure of Inquiry. Harper and Row, 1970.

Pelto, Pertti. The Snowmobile Revolution: Technology and Social Change in the Arctic. Cummings, 1973.

Perfect, Timothy and Bennett L. Schwartz (Editors). Applied Metacognition. University of Cambridge, 2002.

Peters, Arno. Die Neue Kartographie/The New Cartography (in German and English).

Prahalad, C.K., and Kenneth Lieberthal. "The End of Corporate Imperialism." Harvard Business Review, July-August, 1998.

Reck, Gregory. In The Shadow of Tlaloc: Life in a Small Mexican Village. Penguin, 1978.

Report of the World Commission on Forests and Sustainable Development. Our Forests. Cambridge University Press, 1999.

Sahlins, Marshall. "Remarks on Social Structure in Southeast Asia." *Journal of the Polynesian Society*, 1963.

Senge, Peter. The Fifth Discipline. Doubleday, 1990.

Schein, Edgar. Organizational Culture and Leadership. Jossey-Bass, 1985.

Schein, Edgar. The Corporate Culture Survival Guide. Jossey-Bass, 1992.

Schein, Edgar. Dec is Dead: Long Live Dec. Berrett-Koehler, 2003.

Scheinker, Jan and Alan Scheinker. Metacognitive Approach to Social Skills Training. Jones and Bartlett, 1988.

Schrage, Michael. Serious Play. Harvard Business School Press, 2000.

Srivasta, Suresh and Associates (Editors). The Executive Mind. Jossey-Bass, 1983.

Stacey, Ralph. Complexity and Creativity in Organizations. Berrett-Koehler, 1996.

Story, Brad. "Reinventing Everyday Life." *Newsweek*, October 27, 2003.

Tichy, Noel. The Leadership Engine: How Winning Companies Build Leaders at Every Level. HarperBusiness, 1997.

Trompenaars, Fons. Riding the Waves of Culture Change: Understanding Diversity in Global Business. McGraw Hill, 1997.

Tzu, Sun (James Clavell Editor). The Art of War. Dell. 1983.

Vaill, Peter. Managing as a Performing Art. Jossey-Bass, 1989, pg. 2.

van der Heijden, Kees. Scenarios: The Art of Strategic Conversations. Wiley, 2005.

Wheatley, Margaret. Leadership and the New Science. Berrett-Koehler, 1992.

Web References

www.henry-davis.com/MAPS/LMwebpages/257.html.

http://memory-alpha.org/wiki/Prime_Directive, or

http://rescomp.stanford.edu/~cheshire/EinsteinQuotes.html

http://solveclimatenews.com/news/20100223/deforestation-pushing-amazon-its-ecological-limits.

http://www.computing.dcu.ie/~hruskin/RM2.htm

http://www.discoverychannel.co.in/earth/fire/rainforest_fires/index.shtml

http://www.IDEO.com

http://www.indiana.edu/~wanthro/eco.html.

http://www.kaplaneduneering.com/kappnotes/index.php/2010/08/definition-metacognition/

http://www.nationalgeographic.org/maps/

http://www.youtube.com/watch?v=4mH-L6UCCAE.

Subject Index

A
Adaptive challenges, 31
AMC, 177-184
Anthropologists, 22, 24, 25, 45, 57
Anthropology and business, 59, 60, 72
Anthropological research, 121-123
Authority, 31-32

B
Bias, 111
Business complexity, 1
Balcony, 45

C
Change and culture, 58
Complexity, 1, 31, 76
Complexity and performance, 81
Crucibles, 26
Cultural dynamics, 174, 180
Cultural systems, 97-99
Culture, assumptions, values and norms, artifacts, 60-62
Culture and business

performance, 62-63
Culture (defined), 57
Culture studies, 76-80

D
Dis-equilibrium, 32

E
Emergent situations, 33, 35-38
Emic and etic, 125-127, 129, 131
Ethnocentrism, 112
Espoused theories, 100
Ethnography, 123
Equilibrium, 38

F
Fieldwork, 62-63
Filtering, 152
Five Insights, 72
Five Insights Diagnostic Survey, 192-194
Five Insights patterns and sequences, 195-201

G
Generation X, 128
Gladwell hours, 82
Globalization, 9-10, 20-21

Grounded theory, 126

I
Influencing culture, 102-104
Inside and outside analysis, 124
Integration processes, 181
Interviewing, 136-138, 140

J
Journaling, 184
Juxtaposition, 162

K
KAMCO Enterprises, 180-184
KMO, 183-184

L
Leader's new role, 44-45
Leading and anthropology, 131-132
Leadership and complexity and uncertainty, 30
Leadership in emergent situations, 38, 45-47
Leadership pipeline, 30
Leadership (successful), 82
Leadership (transition from management), 29
Leadership work, 28

Learning lab, 74-75
Listening posts, 155

M
Managerial work, 25, 28
Management (skills needed), 26
Management (transition to), 25-26, 36
Managing the news, 157
Maps, 7-9, 11
Mechanistic/Newtonian work, 33-34, 41, 44
Messes, 104
Metacognition, 192
Methodology (research), 123

N
Newtonian view, 33
New Sciences, 31
Novelty, change and complexity, 1

O
Observation, 84, 87-88
Outliers, 81

P
Participant observation, 121, 123, 135-139

Perspective, 14
Perspective (lack of), 14-16
Perspective (maintaining), 17
Perspective and mastery, 210;
Perspective, leadership and
culture, 57
Prime Directive, 104-105

Q
Qualitative research, 123
Quick fix, 44

R
Research, 122

S
Sailboaters and Speedboaters,
75
Significance, 85-86
Simplicity and complexity, 76
Sociogram, 106-108
Systems, 171-173

T
Theoretical sampling, 152-155,
157, 165
Theories in use, 100
Three Situations, 34

U
Uncertainty, 7
Unscheduled visits, 161

W
Whitewater, 33, 39-40

Name Index

Ackoff, Russell, 170, 173, 174
Ames, Daniel, 144
Argysis, Chris, 100
Auerback, Carl, 166
Bell, Cecil, 111
Bell, Chip, 167
Benedict, Ruth, 160
Bennett, John, 109
Bennis, Warren, 48
Berg, Bruce, 144
Bernard, Russell, 89
Bolman, Lee, 66
Bunker, Kerry, 30
Cane, Kwai Chaing, 57
Capra, Fritjof, 171
Chanda, Nayan, 10
Charah, Ram 29
Clapton, Eric, 51
Connor, Daryl, 110
Connors, Roger, 63
Cowan, John, 75
Cummins, H.J., 144
Daniels, Albi, 145
Deal, Terrance, 59, 63
De Geus, Arie, 49
Delta Ailines,34-39

Drotter, Stephen, 29
Dunlosky, John, 203
Einstein, Albert, 13
Eoyang, Glenda, 31
Fetterman, David, 144
Flick, Uwe, 144
French, Wendell, 188
Friedman, Thomas, 9, 10, 18, 20
Gates, Bill, 81, 82
Geertz, Clifford, 61
Gharajedaghi, Jamshid, 171, 172
Gioja, Linda, 31
Gladwell, Malcolm, 81, 82
Glasser, Barney, 126
Hales, Colin, 166
Heifitz, Ronald, 32, 45, 46
Hoebel, E. Adamson, 57
Jet Blue, 3
Kaufman, Draper, 172
Kennedy, Alan, 63, 59
Kerns, Virginia, 186
Kiste, Robert, 58
Kirk, Jerome, 89
Kluger, Jeffrey, 76
Kotter, John, 63
Lao-Tse, 234

Leiberthal, Kenneth, 130
Leung, Kwo, 144
Licke, Brian, 144
Locke, Karen, 144
Lombardo, Michael, 29
Lopez, Barry, 156
Madison, Soyini, 144
McCall, Morgan. Jr., 29
McCall, Morgan W., 29
McGuinn, Roger, 68
Metcalfe, Janet, 203
Millemann, Mark, 31
Miller, Marc, 89
Mirocha, John, 174
Morris, Michael, 144
Moeeison, Ann, 29
Mouawad, Jad, 37
Noel, James, 29
Northwest Airlines, 34-39
Olson, Edwin, 37
Oshry, Barry, 187
Pascale, Richard, 38
Pelto, Pertti, 58, 121
Perfect, Timothy, 203
Peters, Arno, 8, 9
Pike, Kenneth, 144
Prahalad, C.K., 130
Reck, Gregory, 58, 101
Republic Airlines, 34

Russell, Bernard, 89
Ryan, Gerry, 39
Sahlins, Marshal, 61
Saresh Srivasta and
Associates, 27
Schein, Edgar, 59, 159
Scheinker, Alan, 113
Scheinker, Jan, 113
Schon, David, 100
Schrage, Michael, 49
Scott, John, 113
Senge, Peter, 31
Silverstein, Louise, 167
Smith, Tom, 63
Southwest Airlines, 35
Stacey, Ralph, 31, 33
Star Trek, 113
Stone, Brad, 51
Strauss, Anselm, 126
Swartz, Bennett, 203
The Beatles, 81
Tichy, Noel, 29
Trompenaars, Fons, 60
Trudeau, Peirre Elliot, 90
Uys, James, 102
Vaill, Peter, 29, 39, 40
Van der Heijden, Kees, 49
Von Bertalanffy, Ludwig, 171
Wheatly, Margaret, 31

Wilde, Oscar, 115
Wilson, Larry, 40

Zappa, Frank, 58
Zawacki, Robert, 188

About the Author

John Mirocha is the President of John Mirocha & Associates, Inc., a consulting firm that helps businesses create clear, shared direction and design and implement changes that will bring greater purpose and resilience to the firm (www.johnmirocha.com). The organization specializes in three areas: strategy development, change management and leadership development. A special emphasis of John's work is increasing the capability of the business and individuals to become more change adaptive. John is also a Partner at ShareOn Corporate Leader Resources (www.goShareOn.com). In addition to his work as a consultant, John is a Participating Adjunct Professor of Management and Organization at the University of St. Thomas in Minneapolis where he teaches courses in strategic thinking, scenario planning and organizational behavior and change. He received his Ph.D. in Anthropology and Education from the University of Minnesota. Prior to developing his consulting practice, John managed World Wide Learning and Development for one of the world's largest family-held firms.

John has written several articles on corporate culture and change, organizational development, evaluation research and was the Senior Editor of a series of books on systems thinking and human systems, Systems I and Systems II. He is the creator of the Survey of Successful Change Leadership Practices, CAS, http://www.johnmirocha.com/html/cas.htm. John has traveled widely and has worked extensively in Europe, Asia and the Pacific Rim and Latin America as well as Canada and the U.S. He has developed unique insights into many of today's toughest management dilemmas because of his academic preparation in anthropology, his international work, his years of teaching MBA and Executive MBA students and his work as an advisor, process guide and educator for his clients.

"A leader is best when people barely know he exists. Not so good when people obey and acclaim him. Worse when they despise him. But of a good leader, who talks little, when his work is done, his aim fulfilled this they will say, "We did it ourselves."

Lao-Tse (565 B.C.)

Made in the USA
Charleston, SC
05 June 2013